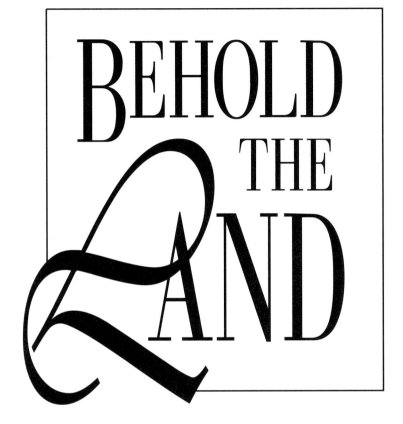

BEHOLD THE LAND

J. B. NICHOLSON JR.

GOSPEL FOLIO PRESS
P. O. Box 2041, Grand Rapids MI 49501-2041
Available in the UK from
JOHN RITCHIE LTD., Kilmarnock, Scotland

Most of this material was originally published in *Counsel* magazine in a column entitled "Landmarks." Other chapters are reprinted from *Uplook* magazine. Some articles appear here for the first time.

Cover and book design by J. B. Nicholson Jr.

MAIN PHOTO CREDITS:
Doug Dixon, pp. 24, 53, 56, 61, 72, 83; J. B. Nicholson Jr., pp. 12, 32, 67, 87; Mendel Nun, p. 28; C. Raad, p. 44; A. T. Schofield, p. 46; Kevin Shantz, pp. 21, 42, 80; Scott Tucker, pp. 38, 76.

INSET PHOTO CREDITS:
Doug Dixon, pp. 15, 16, 18; Roy Gustafson, p. 56; J. B. Nicholson Jr., pp. 12, 21, 32, 59, 67, 80, 81; Kevin Shantz, pp. 26, 38; Scott Tucker, p. 64.

COVER: Spring flowers spread a colorful blanket up to the double-arched Golden Gate in the eastern wall of Jerusalem. Photo by Roy Gustafson.

Published by
Gospel Folio Press, P. O. Box 2041, Grand Rapids, MI 49501-2041

ISBN 1-882701-23-2

Printed in the United States of America

To Louise,
Beloved Companion,
Gracious Advisor,
Fellow Pilgrim on the road Home,
and to our rich Heritage from the Lord:
John, Elisabeth, Moira, Sharon,
Andrea, David & Sara

"Behold the Land"

DEUTERONOMY 32:49

Blest land of Israel! hallowed in song,
Where the holiest of memories, pilgrim-like, throng;
In the shade of thy palms, by the shores of thy sea,
On the hills of thy beauty, my heart is with thee.

Lo, Bethlehem's hill-site before me is seen,
With the mountains around and the valleys between;
There rested the shepherds of Judah, and there
The news of the angels rose sweet on the air.

Blue sea of the hills! in my spirit I hear
Thy waters, Gennesaret, chime on my ear;
Where the Lowly and Just with the people sat down,
And thy spray on the dust of His sandals was thrown.

And Bethany's trees in their beauty still shed
Their shadows at noon on the traveller's head;
But where are the sisters who hastened to greet
The lovely Redeemer, and sit at His feet?

I tread where the twelve in their wayfaring trod;
I stand where they stood with the chosen of God;
Where His blessings were heard, and His lessons were taught,
Where the blind were restored, and the healings were wrought.

Oh, here with His flock the sad Wanderer came;
These hills He toiled over in grief are the same;
The founts where He drank by the wayside still flow,
And the same airs are blowing which breathed on His brow.

But what if my feet may not tread where He stood,
Nor my ears hear the dashing of Galilee's flood,
Nor my eyes see the hill where He bowed Him to bear,
Nor my knees press Gethsemane's garden in prayer?

Yet, loved of the Father, Thy Spirit is near
To the meek, and the lowly, and penitent here;
And the voice of Thy love is the same even now
As at Bethany's tomb or on Olivet's brow.

—JOHN GREENLEAF WHITTIER

Contents

Tables of Maps & Photographs

Foreword

"Behold the land" was the word given to God's great servant, Moses, as the children of Israel at last reached the borders of Canaan. He was to climb Mount Nebo and, from that vantage, he would view the Land of Promise. Not only from that range, but also from the edge of eternity, for there on that mountain he would die, and God would be his pallbearer.

What were his thoughts as his eyes swept the panorama of the country to which he had led the people these forty years—but would not enter with them? He was not just scanning the majesty of her mountains and the beauty of her lush valleys, but all that lay before him in the sweep of history. Did he recall Abraham, mighty in faith, and the covenant to give him a seed and a land—this land? Did the Lord give His great servant Moses a foregleam of the glory that one day will shine upon His people in that land, as never before? Did he see in the distance the Lamb of God that would forever set aside the blood-stained altars of the levitical order he had brought down to the people from Sinai?

So it is for all who would "behold the land" even today. As soon as we arrive, we are at once impressed that this is not just a conglomeration of hills and of valleys, of rivers and of rocks, but of the Lord God coming down to dwell among a people He would call "My people." The tourist may see only the delineation of the land, be amazed at the descent to Jericho and bask in the luxury of elite hotels, but not the Bible student. In this land he sees the spread of history from eternity to eternity. The rocks yield up the evidence of a God who would not give up on His people though they so often forsook Him and His ways—and suffered terribly as a result. Yet He would give, and keep on giving until He could give no more, opening the flood-gates of His love and "gave His only begotten Son." What a story! What a land! What a people!

It was late, and the young waitress was clearing up the tables on the hotel patio that overlooks Gennesaret. As we spoke with her and shared in the wonder of the history of her people and the glorious future that awaits them—but not without sorrow—her eyes brimmed up and the tears spilled down her cheeks, "I...didn't know," she faltered. We told her how we were but *goyim*. We had been in the place of no covenant, no hope, and without God in the world. As we told her how we have been brought out of our darkness to worship the God of Israel, to love and to serve Him, but as such a cost to Him to make it so, she was obviously moved. We told her of the Lamb of God in anguish bearing away the sins of the world, the One who loved her—and us all—passionately, personally. He was the Man of sorrows, the acquaintance of grief. He was "wounded for our transgressions," as prophesied by Isaiah. And the recovered record is there in the Shrine of the Book in Jerusalem for all to see. I still remember her name because it is often breathed in prayer to God that she may enter by faith into an inheritance "that fadeth not away."

No, you can never be quite the same again after you "behold the land." For those of us privileged to have been there and for many who have not, the author of *Behold the Land* has done a signal and diligent service in preparing this book. His numerous visits, his grasp of the weaving of Scripture with the geography and history of the Land, the people and the earth-shaking events both past and yet to come, helps to make this book a treasure-trove for the student and a delight for the occasional reader. It will thrill those who know the land and those who have never been there.

However, a word of warning is appropriate. The reading of this book may be dangerous to your wallet! Once you have read it and revelled in the wonder of God's ways in the Land and with its people, you may be on the next tour that the author will lead to Israel, if the Lord will.

I would normally call the author by his given name. It happens to be the same as mine. You see, his mother and I gave it to him the day he was born.

J. BOYD NICHOLSON
ST. CATHARINES, ONTARIO

Photo: *The southern flank of the Hill of Moreh, site of Gideon's nighttime attack on the Midianites (from Jezreel).*
Inset: *Ein Harod, the spring flowing from the base of Mt. Gilboa, where Gideon's 300 minutemen were chosen.*

Introduction

*Y*ou hear about it weekly in the news. You read about it daily in your Bible. It is the only place on the planet where the incarnate God traversed its serpentine roads, its ancient hills, and slept upon its bosom under a canopy of stars. It is Eretz Israel—the land of the Bible. And if you are a believer in heaven's great plan, you know that Jehovah is not finished with this little piece of real estate at the eastern end of the Mediterranean. You know that His promises to Abraham and David were no idle boasts. The God who cannot lie intends to fulfill every word of them.

Some say the land of Israel is nothing more than the barren stage upon which the drama of the ages was enacted. Mere props, they tell us, these rocks and rivers, these sun-kissed vineyards and windswept peaks and lonely deserts. It does seem strange, if that is so, that there is so much geography mentioned in the Bible. Would *any* mountain have done when Jehovah called Abraham to offer his son? Why, then, did He send him three days' hard journey past a score of mountains to that "mountain I will tell thee of"? Did it matter the town in which the Lord Jesus would pass from boy to man? Why then should it be prophesied that He would be called the Nazarene? What is it about Shechem and Joppa, Mount Tabor and the Valley of Armageddon, in fact, of every place mentioned on purpose by the Spirit of God, that makes them not simply the backdrops to the events that occur there, but an integral element in the stories themselves? This volume suggests that historical geography is a key to many precious truths in the Bible. We will watch as the Spirit of God skillfully weaves together the warp of biblical geography with the woof of its history. The finished tapestry is breathtaking.

To "behold" means more than a passing glance, a furtive look. The Old English *behealdan* means just that—to be held by something, to have one's attention held, captivated. Surely the territory traversed by patriarchs, prophets, warriors, kings, apostles and martyrs—to say nothing of Immanuel Himself—ought to be a place that would cause us to scrutinize every detail. I invite you to *Behold the Land* with me.

Even a humble effort like this involves the aid of many. I have had the privilege of taking several hundred Bible students to learn in the Land. Their questions and comments have been invaluable in my own study. Their fellowship has been as sweet as it comes this side of heaven. I have also learned much from Phillip Halperin, my perennial guide. To him I owe more than I can express. We have shared much of the Word of God; I look forward to the day when we shall be able to share it all.

Special thanks to the State of Israel and the people of every race who live there. I and my fellow-pilgrims appreciate your hospitality, your sharing of the incomparable richness of the country, and for your patient bearing with us as we tramp across your hills and valleys, singing, learning, never to be the same.

I have benefitted greatly from many books on the subject, but especially from Barry Beitzel's *Moody Atlas of Bible Lands,* J. Howard Kitchen's *Holy Fields,* J. W. Clapham's *Palestine, The Land of My Adoption,* John Phillips' *Exploring the World of the Jew,* and Charles Gulston's *Jerusalem: the Tragedy and the Triumph.*

To O. B. and Mary Ann Snider I owe a debt of gratitude for giving me my first taste of the land flowing with milk and honey. It is evident I never got over it. To Roy Gustafson, my first teacher in Israel, sincerest of thanks. And to the faithful staff of Gospel Folio Press—especially Caroline Cairns, Doug Dixon, Deborah Lein, Kevin Shantz, and Scott Tucker—my gratitude!

How can I thank my dear partner in life, Louise, for her example of pilgrim living, her encouragement, and for graciously allowing me the time for reading, writing, and visiting in Israel. To John, Beth, and Moira—who have taken the journey with me—and to Sharon, Andrea, David, and Sara—who await their turn to go—you certainly know how to make this father feel deeply grateful to the Lord.

To the Creator of the Ages, one-time Babe at Bethlehem, Carpenter from Nazareth, Teacher by Galilee, Saviour of Calvary, soon-returning Bridegroom, coming King of Glory, to Him be all the praise.

J. B. NICHOLSON, JR.
GRAND RAPIDS, MICHIGAN

With an Eagle's Eye

*B*efore we look in detail at the places in Israel which are the settings for history's great events, it would be helpful to rise on eagle's wings high above the land. Looking down from our vantage-point, we immediately notice three things. First, we see, between the brilliant blue of the Mediterranean and the blanched hues of the desert, a narrow swath of green swinging away to the southwest and northeast. It is easy to see how it received its name, "the Fertile Crescent." We are looking at the cradle of human civilization. The barren desert is never far away and is always ready to encroach, but there is this pleasant green exception formed by the Nile River in Egypt, the Tigris and Euphrates Rivers in Mesopotamia, and the Jordan River (plus seasonal rains) in Israel.

The two super-powers of the ancient world were at either end of this arc. For two millennia they struggled back and forth with Canaan as the battlefield—and the winner's prize. It is evident that, apart from faith in God and His preserving care, the Israelites became mere pawns in a giant chess game.

We notice, too, that Israel forms a land bridge between Europe, Africa, and Asia, the three old-world continents. It could be worth your life to cross the Arabian Desert. So Abram was not detouring when he went by way of Haran to Canaan; he was following the safe, river valley route. Because land movements were funnelled through what is known as the Levant, what a wonderful way to bring the world to your door! If Jehovah wanted His people to be a witness to the nations concerning the true God, there could be no better place for "walk-in" converts than here. Unfortunately, like many of God's people today, the world with its passing fancies and little gods converted Israel to their thinking instead of Israel convincing the world.

The third characteristic that draws our attention from this bird's-eye view is its exceeding smallness. It is not hard to imagine Abraham on the heights of Hebron or Moses on Nebo seeing the scope of the promise on a clear day. From Dan, under the shadow of Mount Hermon in the north, to Beersheba on the edge of the Negev in the south, it is only 150 miles (240 km.). It is hardly more than 50 miles (80 km.) from Joppa on the Mediterranean Sea to Jericho in the Jordan Valley. Yet this land, the size of the country of Wales or the state of New Jersey, was big enough to pour into it the promises of God, and to manifest the glory of God, especially in the face of its Heavenly Stranger, the Lord Jesus Christ.

Its landforms, while having a certain winsomeness, can hardly compare with much of the earth's beauty. Its material culture was not notable. Its distinctive architecture (not that borrowed from the Greeks or Romans) would draw little attention. Its surviving art and literature, apart from the Bible, has made little impact. Yet this mere speck on a world map has had more influence on the human race than any other civilization in history. Law, morals, ethics, religion, finance, statesmanship, music, poetry, language, and more recently agriculture, military strategy and hardware, and scientific discoveries have flowed from this little land and its people to encompass the whole world.

Like the waves that ebb and flow upon the Mediterranean coast, the borders of the land of Israel have shifted with the tides of time. Immigration, famines, wars, and economic expansion have all played their part in the redrawing of the shape of Canaan. The land is divided topographically by four strips running north and south. Let us begin at the sea, and move east:

1) *The coastal plain,* 190 miles from the Ladder of Tyre to Wadi el-Arish. This includes the plains of Asher (as far south as Carmel), Dor (from Carmel to the Crocodile swamps), Sharon (from the swamps to the Yarkon River), and Philistia (south from the Yarkon). Through it traveled the Great Trunk Road between Egypt and Europe. Ironically, this territory which Israel found impossible to hold in Bible times was the land given to them by United Nations partitioning in 1948.

2) *The central mountain spine,* included the Galilean, Samaritan, Judean, and Negev ranges, is only pierced by the Jezreel Valley. These ranges vary in altitude from 1,500 feet to 3,300 feet above sea level. It was in these mountains that most of Israel's fortress cities were built.

3) *The rift valley* includes the Jordan River, the Sea of Galilee, and the Dead Sea. This is part of the

The dome of Mount Tabor looms over the Jezreel Valley, from which Deborah and Barak descended against Sisera and "led captivity captive" in a graphic prefiguring of our Lord's glorious victory (see Eph. 4)

longest (¹⁄₆ of the earth's circumference), deepest, and widest faults in the earth's surface.

4) *The eastern plateau* is simply called in the Bible "beyond Jordan." This tableland (alt. 5,000 feet) is 30-80 miles wide and stretches 250 miles from Mount Hermon to the Dead Sea.

In Bible times, the land was also divided politically into four areas, each running east and west:

1) North of the Jezreel was "Galilee of the Gentiles" (because of its non-Israelite population). Here our Lord lived and ministered.

2) Samaria, "the hill country of Ephraim," took its name from the capital of Israel. After the Assyrian invasion, it was populated by others from abroad (2 Ki. 17) and though they intermarried and embraced some Judaisms, they were rejected by Israel. Some 350 still live nearby and celebrate Passover on "this mountain," as the Samaritan woman referred to it in speaking to the Lord Jesus.

3) Judea played a key role in the history of the land—the patriarchs, Melchizedek, Caleb, Othniel, Ehud, Samson, Saul and Jonathan, David and Solomon, and later Isaiah, Jeremiah, Daniel and others trekked across her landscape. But it was only after David took Jerusalem from the Jebusites that Judea became the hub of Israeli national life.

4) Edom (or Idumea) was an ill-defined region wrapping around the south end of the Dead Sea resulting from the Edomites immigrating out of the way of the Nabateans. One of these Idumeans was Herod the Great and the evil brood he spawned.

In seeking to determine the borders of the land promised to the children of Israel, one is faced with two major difficulties: 1) *The Time Factor:* The boundaries are obviously going to vary according to period. 2) *The Place Factor:* While the major boundaries were based on easy-to-find natural borders, the locations of some key cities on the perimeter are not always certain.

The simplest border to fix is the western (Num. 34:6; Josh. 15:47; Ezek. 47:20), which followed the Mediterranean (the Great Sea, or simply "the sea"). The Lord gave Israel the whole coast from the river of Egypt (probably Wadi el-Arish) in the south to approximately 70 miles north of the city of Beirut. But much of the southern plain (the Gaza Strip) was in the hands of the Philistines, while the north was held by the Phoenicians.

The northern border (Num. 34:7-9; Josh. 19:17-39; Ezek. 47:15-17; 48:1-7) probably followed a natural boundary, the el-Kabir valley, at the northern end of the Lebanon mountains, past the Lake of Homs, then east to the Syrian Desert, approximately 75 miles north of Damascus.

The eastern border encompassed the territories taken from Sihon and Og (Deut. 2 & 3) including the lands of Mishor, Gilead, and Bashan (the Golan Heights) but not including the territories of Edom, Moab, and Ammon. Thus the border skirted the Syrian desert, encompassing the headwaters of the Yarmuk, Jabbok, and Arnon Rivers. Moab shared the southeast part of the Dead Sea.

The southern border (Num. 34:3-5; Josh. 15:1-4; Ezek. 47:19) is easier to determine. If one agrees that the river of Egypt is Wadi el-Arish, then it joins four other points known with some certainty: the Dead Sea, the Wilderness of Zin (today called the high Negev), and Kadesh-barnea. This forms a shallow vee with the Ramon uplands on the southeast arm, Mount Kharif at the apex, and Wadi el-Arish forming the southwest arm with Kadesh-barnea at its source.

Leaving now the more technical aspects of the land behind, we will take our time meandering through the miles and the millennia that have woven across Eretz Israel's bosom a tapestry more fascinating than any other place on the planet.

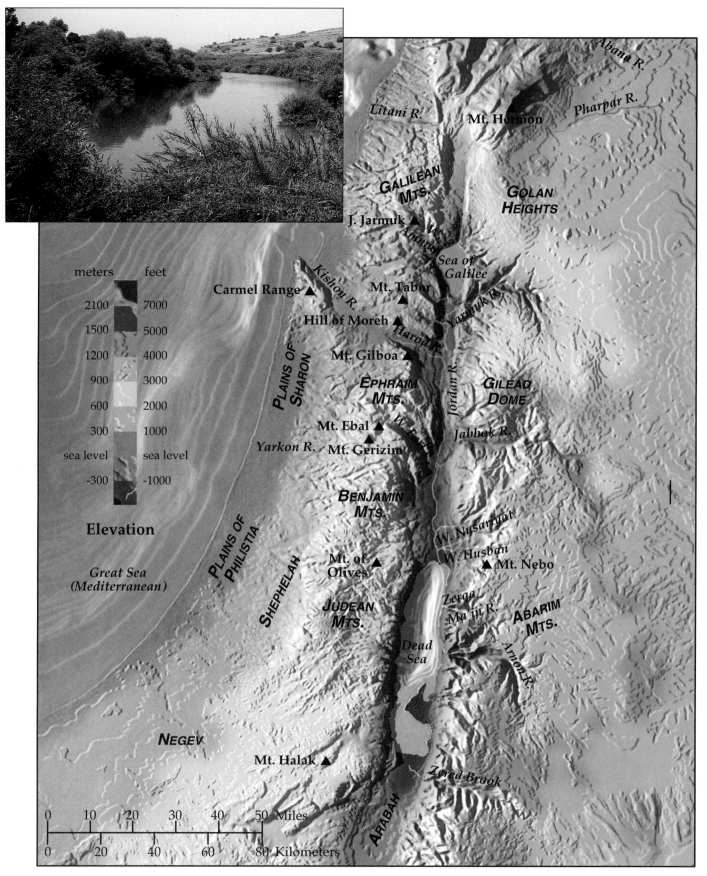

meters	feet
2100	7000
1500	5000
1200	4000
900	3000
600	2000
300	1000
sea level	sea level
-300	-1000

Elevation

Great Sea
(Mediterranean)

Abana R.

Litani R.

Mt. Hermon

Pharpar R.

GALILEAN
MTS.

GOLAN
HEIGHTS

J. Jarmuk ▲

Amana

Sea of
Galilee

Carmel Range ▲

Kishon R.

Mt. Tabor ▲

Hill of Moreh ▲

Harod R.

Yarmuk R.

Mt. Gilboa ▲

PLAINS OF
SHARON

EPHRAIM
MTS.

GILEAD
DOME

Jordan R.

Mt. Ebal ▲

W. Far'ah

Jabbok R.

Yarkon R.

Mt. Gerizim ▲

BENJAMIN
MTS.

W. Nusariyat

PLAINS OF
PHILISTIA

SHEPHELAH

Mt. of
Olives ▲

W. Husban

▲ Mt. Nebo

JUDEAN
MTS.

Zerqa
Ma'in R.

ABARIM
MTS.

Dead
Sea

NEGEV

Arnon R.

Mt. Halak ▲

Zered Brook

ARABAH

0   10   20   30   40   50   Miles

0   20   40   60   80   Kilometers

Map: *Showing the elevation and waterways in the land of Israel.*
Inset: *The Upper Jordan River just north of the Sea of Galilee. The river is already 500 feet below sea level at this point.*

An Armchair Visit

*I*t's already dark as our 747 thunders in over the Israeli coast at Tel Aviv. We're here to explore the land that is like no other. I never intended on coming even once (pre-rapture) to the land of Abraham, Isaac, and Jacob. My first trip to Israel, with my wife, was a gift from friends who wanted to invest in our ministry. I had no idea what it would do for my Bible study. But once I saw the help I could gain from being here, I was quick to encourage others to go.

As we traverse the dusty hills and crowded bypaths of the land, I can almost see Nehemiah walking the ramparts of old Zion or Elijah praying down heaven's pyrotechnics at Carmel. And there are just some things you can't put into words: like the brook chortling its way over the rocks at the Spring of Harod where Gideon's minutemen were selected, or the wind in the myrtles still growing along Emek Rephaim, a sound that was the sure sign of victory for David in his hour of need.

I never get over the eerie desolation of the Judean wilderness, the haunting spell that catches me in my throat and mists my eyes by sweet Galilee, or the breathtaking blanket of spring flowers—especially the scarlet Crown Anemone and the florescent yellow Wild Mustard in the springtime. And how can you, without having been there, catch the lively smells of the spices wafting from an Arab souk, or believe the blazing reds and purples of Moses' Nebo at sunset, or understand the thrill of musing at Gethsemane, or—dare I say it—singing at Calvary?

In spite of the shortness of the trip ahead, the dizzying pace, and the information coming at you so fast you feel you're trying to drink at a fire hydrant, the whole experience is nothing less than exhilarating. But I warn you: it may be habit-forming! Meeting the people who live there, talking about life's important things to Jews and Arabs, locals and pilgrims, visiting the very sites where some of history's key events occurred—it is the journey of a lifetime.

Of course, you don't have to travel seven time zones away to understand your Bible. It is far more important to walk *as* our Lord walked than *where* He walked. Much better to look forward to being *where He is* than seeing *where He was.* True, all true. However…

Come with me on this journey to get a taste at least of such a tour through the land of Israel from Dan to Beersheba, from Joppa to Jericho, from Bethlehem to Olivet. It is, as I say, only a taste. But it might stimulate your appetite, if not for a journey to Israel, at least for a more serious study of the geography of the Bible, a more vigorous prayer investment for the people who live there, and a greater desire to see the Lord reign there in the day that "the earth shall be filled with the knowledge of the glory of the Lord, as the waters cover the sea" (Hab. 2:14).

Of course you should go to Israel, and you will go—sooner or later, if you have placed your trust in Heaven's Lamb. The way world events are looking, it probably will be sooner than later. As one worker in the land said to me, "Jerusalem is a cup of trembling. The Lord's coming is surely soon." Maranatha. Come quickly, Lord!

But in the meantime, let us be actively engaged in following the Shepherd of Bethlehem's fields, serving the Fisherman of Capernaum's shore, learning from the Teacher of Olivet's mount, living for the Saviour of Golgotha's tree, and waiting for the Bridegroom of Cana's new wine.

Now come with me and see what we can learn in the land.

Your Tour Host

J B Nichols

Two Guides for the Journey

On several trips to Israel over the years, I have been privileged to have as my guide a gracious and well-informed Jew, named at birth Phillip Halperin. Phillip was the name of one of the kings of Romania, and it was not a wise thing to give Hebrew names to little Jewish boys in wartime Europe. It could be dangerous for their health.

Phillip Halperin was one of the fortunate ones. His family was able to escape. Making their way to Palestine, however, they were stopped by the British blockade and sent to a detention camp on Cyprus until the end of the British mandate in Israel.

Finally settled in their homeland, little Phillip began attending school. "Phillip?" queried the teacher, looking down at the little fellow who had already lived a lifetime in the span of his few years. "That's not a Jewish name! From now on, you will be Yechiel." And so it was.

Yechiel means *Long Live God*. Fortunately, in a world full of worry, that is not one of the issues we need be concerned about. Our God not only is the possessor of eternal life, but the giver of such life to all who seek it from Him. But the life of God seems so remote, so unlike the life we have, or even the life we need for our earthly pilgrimage. If only we could see such a life up close—a life that could weep, yet smile through the tears and find a certain hope beyond the grave. If only there was someone like us (and yet unlike us) who could walk with us and talk of God in such a way that we could know this One who dwells in unapproachable glory.

Moses longed for this. "He said, I beseech Thee, show me Thy glory" (Ex. 33:18). But the Lord could show him only the afterglow as he hid in the cleft of the rock for, said the Lord, "Thou canst not see My face: for there shall no man see Me, and live" (v. 20). Job desired a daysman "that might lay his hand upon us both" because God, said Job, "is not a man, as I am" (Job 9:32–33).

David cried, "Bow Thy heavens, O Lord, and come down" (Ps. 144:5), as did Isaiah: "Oh that Thou wouldest rend the heavens, that Thou wouldest come down" (Isa. 64:1).

At last He did! The King came down, down from His palace to a stable, from a throne to a manger. No longer was it the afterglow, but the "light of the knowledge of the glory of God in the face of Jesus Christ" (2 Cor. 4:6). Not a daysman to lay hands upon us both, but "one mediator between God and men, the man Christ Jesus; who gave Himself a ransom for all" (1 Tim. 2:5–6). He did not rend the heavens in a display of His power, but slipped quietly in among us, making Himself "of no reputation, and took upon Him the form of a servant, and was made in the likeness of men" (Phil. 2:7). So it is that John declares: "God hath given to us eternal life, and this life is in His Son" (1 Jn. 5:11).

As one king succumbs to the Last Enemy and another takes his place on the throne, the cry is heard through the land: "The king is dead. Long live the king." With the best of kings or the worst of kings, it was the same. The scepter slips from their grasp and the sovereign becomes another subject to the King of Terrors. Until this King came.

Phillip Halperin

Born to die, He followed His mission unerringly through life. At last He came to His coronation at the hands of men. They fashioned for His diadem the symbol of the cursed earth, the curse He would bear for them. The royal scarlet He wore was drawn from His back with the lash. And then, alone, He descended into the hideous darkness of death to deliver us from its bondage and blaze a pathway of light into the presence of God.

Standing by the cross, they watched the King die. Over His head His charge had been inscribed: This is Jesus of Nazareth, the King. At last, a shout of triumph, and the King is dead. Heaven, Bethlehem, Nazareth, Galilee, Jerusalem, Gethsemane, Gabbatha, Golgotha, the grave, the glory. Long live the King!

The King has promised to guide His people to His palace-home. It would be the highest folly not to ask Him to take us safely on life's journey. "Walk about Zion, and go round about her: tell the towers thereof. Mark ye well her bulwarks, consider her palaces; that ye may tell it to the generation following. For this God is our God for ever and ever: He will be our guide even unto death" (Ps. 48:12-14).

The Heights of Hermon

Where should we begin our fascinating journey through the "Holy Fields," as Howard Kitchen called them? It matters little, because wherever one looks he sees a veritable banquet of biblical delights. I shall begin in the extreme northern reaches of the land, at the place where today the countries of Syria, Lebanon, and Israel touch. Although David's and Solomon's kingdoms extended far to the north of Hermon, it was land that was subjugated, but never settled, by the Israelites. The traditional northern extent of inhabited Canaan was the city of Dan under the shadow of the noble Hermon.

There are two mountain ranges that thrust their way down from Syria, like a great pincer grabbing at the headwaters of the Jordan River. The western arm is the Lebanon Range, while the Anti-Lebanon Mountains run parallel to the east, on the other side of the great Beqa' Valley. The southern piece of this eastern range, divided from the main portion by the Abana River, are the peaks of Mount Hermon.

More than sixteen miles long, the highest peak of the range reaches 9,232 feet high. It was called Sirion by the inhabitants of Sidon (Deut. 3:9; Ps. 29:6); Shenir or Senir by the local Amorites (1 Chron. 5:23; Song of Sol. 4:8; Ezek. 27:5); and once called Sion (Deut. 4:48). Today it is called Jebel-esh-Sheikh (mountain of snow) by the Arab population. Receiving an average of 60 inches of annual precipitation, its hoary crown remains white most of the year (Jer. 18:14). There is some discrepancy as to the meaning of the name "Hermon," which occurs eleven times in the Old Testament. Some say it means "prominent," others "rugged," and still others "sanctuary." But there should be no discrepancy to the statement that Hermon is all three. It is certainly prominent. The highest mountain in the Anti-Lebanons, they say that a sharp eye can see the summit from the Frank Mountain near Bethlehem (80 miles away) on a clear day.

Regarding its dominating influence, C. R. Conder wrote: "Mt. Hermon is the most conspicuous feature in the scenery of Palestine…There are three low peaks on the top, with a connecting plateau. Lower down, the sides are covered with vineyards round the Druze villages. On the sandstone to the west there are still pines and firs, but the upper part is quite barren…The view from the top is magnificent…"

Although its southern flank was part of the inheritance of Manasseh, some from the tribe of Dan felt they knew better than the Lord (a folly not restricted to those ancient days) and, leaving their strategic location only a few miles from Jerusalem, they established their colony near Hermon at Laish (renamed Dan). Now it was easier to make an excuse rather than an effort to attend the worship of the Lord at the temple, so they were the first to institutionalize idolatry in Israel. It was here that, fourteen centuries later, the One seeking worshippers for His Father and a Bride for His heart, announced the plan to build from Jews and Gentiles a Church that could withstand armed combat with hell itself. He knew what it would cost: "Jesus began to show unto His disciples, how that He must…suffer many things of the elders and chief priests and scribes, and be killed, and be raised again the third day" (Mt. 16:21).

It would seem appropriate, then, that the Transfiguration took place here rather than at Tabor or elsewhere. It was in the immediate location of Caesarea Philippi. It was isolated (Tabor was not, having a Roman garrison crowding its top—Josephus was stationed there). How suitable if it was on the mount whose name means "set apart" where they saw "Jesus only," and His raiment became "exceeding white as snow" (Mk. 9:3). But it is very suitable for another reason.

Cascading down its rugged slopes from hundreds of springs is the water that forms the three main sources of the Jordan River—the Baniyas, the Dan, and the Hasbani. In Psalm 133:2-3, David linked blessing, unity, and growth by using two illustrations. He spoke of the precious anointing oil that ran down from the high priest's head to the hem of his garments, bringing fragrance to every part. Then he described the dew upon Hermon that descended to fill the land with blessing—even life for evermore.

See our Great High Priest standing there, speaking of that day when He would pay the mighty price at Calvary to unify the saints, that they would "grow up into Him in all things, which is the head, even Christ: from whom the whole body (right to the hem)…maketh increase of the body unto the edifying of itself in love." "Behold, how good and how pleasant it is for brethren to dwell together in unity."

Descender

Bursting from the southern flank of Mount Hermon and laughing their way through the rocks and tangle of brushwood and ferns are three sources of the Jordan River. A fourth, rising to the northwest, joins the others as they ripple southward toward Lake Hula. The three from Hermon—the Banias, the Dan, and the Hasbani—result from hundreds of springs cascading down the mountainside.

It is not surprising to know that Jordan means *Descender* when one follows the course of the river from the snowy brow of Hermon at 9,232 feet to 300 feet above sea level at Hula, then plunging to Galilee at 700 feet below sea level, the lowest sweet-water lake on earth. But it has only begun to descend. From the south end of the Sea of Galilee to the Dead Sea is only 65 air miles; however, the river manages to traverse more than 200 miles as it meanders through the Zor, the hollowed-out bed in the Jordan Valley. As it empties into the Dead Sea, it is almost 1,300 feet below sea level.

In even a greater sense than England's Thames, the Jordan River can rightly be called "liquid history." Howard Kitchen says of the river, "Strangely enough, for most of us it is not...Father Tiber of the Romans, nor the Holy Ganges of the Hindus, nor the sacred Nile of the Egyptians, that call forth our deepest and most enduring memories, but that narrow, turbid stream in Palestine which lays its head among the snows of Hermon, buries its trunk in a steaming valley and has its feet in a desolate lake without an outlet. The Jordan would carry an easy vote for the world's most memorable river."

Sir George A. Smith writes: "There may be something on the surface of another planet to match the Jordan Valley: there is nothing on this...Is it not true that on the earth there is nothing else like this deep, this colossal ditch?" He adds, "There are hardly less ugly mud banks, from two to twenty feet high...not clean and sparkling as in our rivers, but foul with ooze and slime." Tourists to Israel today are hardly more impressed with the Jordan than Smith was, or Naaman, for that matter. It is not difficult to see why he would have preferred the rivers of his own land. The muddy character of the flow is partly a result of the swiftness of the current due to the rapidity of descent. It is this that has carried the rich deposits into the Dead Sea which have made it a coveted mineral treasure house.

The rate of drop is approximately 40 feet per mile between Galilee and the Dead Sea. But the river is not simply distinctive because "Its origin is peculiar, its flow exactly from north to south; it forms the eastern boundary for the most interesting country in the world; it flows through the lowest depression on the earth's surface, and finally loses itself in the strangest sheet of water in existence" (J. W. Clapham); there is something more, much more.

The patriarchs crossed this river; Elijah and Elisha watched God's power slice open a path for them through it. Gideon and Jephthah took its fords to contain the enemy; David crossed it in exile. Israel passed through on dry ground with the Ark holding back the waters as far as Adam. Is that location coincidence? Fifteen centuries of river rolled its course until the True Ark went down into the Descender (Mt. 3:13-17). Unlike Israel and Elijah and Elisha, the river did not open for Him. All the way back to Adam, the waves would roll over Him when He tasted death for everyone (Rom. 5:12-19).

Ah, but the heavens opened! The Father spoke audibly to Israel for the first time in well-nigh four hundred years. How could He keep silent? "This is My beloved Son," He said. And the Spirit added His sweet Amen as, in dove's form, He alighted upon the head now wet with the Jordan, soon to be wet with His own blood and the filthy spittle of men.

There was a day when David recrossed the Jordan on his way back to Salem and his throne. And there is a day coming when David's Lord will return. Coming from Edom, His garments dipped in blood, He too will recross the Descender, climb the Red Ascent, crest Olivet, and, like the sun breaking on the dark world, will burst upon the city of His erstwhile humiliation with healing in His rays.

Let men dip in the muddy Jordan if they will. Let them carry home their little bottles of its liquid. I will await the day when at last the murky flow from Adam will forever be rolled back, when the Golden Ark will be lifted up by His king-priests for all the world to see.

Photo: *The southern tip of Mount Hermon from which issue three sources of the Jordan River. This is the Banias.*
Inset: *A carved niche (also seen in the large photo, middle right) used for idols at the ancient site of Caesarea Philippi.*

Northern Galilee

With the Golan Heights on the east, the Lebanon Mountains on the north, and the Upper Galilee Range on the west forming a sweeping crescent, the Hula Valley lies like a fertile bowl tipped toward the south. The northern end of the elongated valley is at 230 feet above sea level and the little lake at the southern end just above sea level. Here the headwaters of the Jordan join before the little triangular lake pours its contents into a gorge two miles south. The gorge, cut through black basalt rock, carries the cascading river to the Sea of Galilee, 695 feet below sea level.

The little lake has been known by various names through history. It is called Lake Hula; some maps have it listed by the ungainly name of Lake Semachonitis. It has often been proposed that Lake Hula is the Waters of Merom (meaning *a high place*). An alternate site is Meiron where a spring pours water into the Wadi Meiron, about ten miles northwest of the Galilee.

The region around the lake is lush in vegetation. Bulrushes and papyrus grow in abundance. In Bible days, hyenas, jackals, and boars roamed the marshes. During the time of Turkish occupation (1516-1917), the rivers were left unirrigated and the valley became a malarial swamp—one of the first matters of business for the Israelis in 1948. Young people like Golda Meier and Moshe Dayan slogged in these fields to make them fertile again. It is rich river bottom land. Tickle it with the hoe; watch it grow.

A few miles southwest of the lake was the ancient city of Hazor (pronounced *Hat-sor*, meaning *an enclosed place)*. Hazor was the superpower of the northern Canaanite city-states. When Joshua led the twelve tribes into the Promised Land, it was Jabin, king of Hazor, who led the northern confederacy. His attempt to stop the Galilean encroachment of the Israelites met with dismal failure at the Waters of Merom. Marshalling a score of neighboring armies, Jabin set the rendezvous for this site at the hub of a dozen valleys that radiate like spokes into the surrounding countryside. "With horses and chariots very many" (Josh. 11:4), the armies gathered "even as the sand that is upon the sea shore in multitude."

Joshua's foot soldiers looked paltry by comparison. But of course he had his secret weapon—the almighty Word of God. In dramatic understatement, Jehovah said to Joshua, "Be not afraid because of them; for tomorrow about this time will I deliver them up all slain before Israel." As always, God was as good as His word. By nightfall, all that was left of the once-proud forces of northern Canaan were the flames licking at the ruins of Hazor and the bones of the chariots littering the valley. Jabin was dead, the survivors hiding like frightened animals in the high country. The battle of Merom is given as c. 1394 BC.

Two centuries rolled their course. The walls of Hazor were rebuilt. Another Jabin came to the throne. His military forces boasted 900 chariots of iron (Israel would not enter the Iron Age until the days of David). From the town of Harosheth Ha-goyim, Jabin hired Sisera to be his commander. And with his might he oppressed Israel for twenty years. Israel was disarmed and demoralized.

High up in the Galilean Hills, overlooking the Hula Valley, was the refuge city of Kedesh, the home of a young Israeli named Barak *(lightning)*. Summoned by the prophetess Deborah to her tent in Mount Ephraim, she reminded him of the call of God in his life. Was he not to lead troops against the oppressor? Easier said than done! We armchair generals might find it easy to disdain Barak for his cowardice, but would you take 10,000 ill-equipped men up Mount Tabor to send them, kamikaze-style, down its nearly vertical slopes into the teeth of Sisera's war machine?

In spite of his reticence, God considered Barak's action worthy of a recounting in the annals of Israel's war history (Jud. 4), a duet victory song (Jud. 5), a verse in Israel's national anthem (Ps. 68:18), use as an illustration of the victory at Mount Calvary (Eph. 4), and a place in the Hall of Faith (Heb. 11). We might do well to think twice before we criticize the man.

Being strategically positioned beside the main thoroughfare from Syria, Hazor has been a key to the defense of the land. Solomon made it one of his three chariot cities. Later, Ahab built a massive water system there. And although one cannot see it, near the Hazor tell today are major fortifications for the Israeli Defense Forces—whose commander at the time of writing, by the way, is Ehud Barak.

The Curse and the Blessing

I awaken early to watch the sun spread its rippling sheet of gold across the surface of the Galilean lake. Palm fronds stir in the morning breeze along the edge of this subtropical inland sea. A few fishing boats are pulling into the harbor of Tiberias after a night of toil in the deep. To the south, the Greek cities of the Decapolis once stood in their splendor, now crumbling heaps of stone. To these the Saviour, when He was here, brought the news of Heaven's matchless love. Don't be surprised to meet some of their former inhabitants in Heaven. Across on the eastern side, now called the Golan Heights, are the lands of Gergesa and Gadara, where the Lord worked miracles and saw a few lost sheep come to the arms of the Shepherd. Among them was a demoniac who was liberated from the chains that bound his soul only to be bound by love to his Master. How like the woman from across the lake to the northwest, Mary of Magdala, who, delivered from seven demons, followed her Lord right to His grave—and on to glory.

Today the west, east, and southern shores bustle with activity. But the northern shore, running at an angle from the plains of Gennesaret to the Golan, is strangely silent. During our Saviour's earthly sojourn it was the location of three key cities: Capernaum, Bethsaida, and Chorazin.

Capernaum is the best known of the three, and rightly so, for here the Lord Jesus lived for three-and-a-half years, administering the blessing of Heaven upon its citizenry. Here He healed Peter's mother-in-law, the centurion's servant, the nobleman's son, the man with the withered hand, and many more. Here He commissioned Peter to catch one fish down at the harbor after Peter had answered rashly that, of course, his Master paid temple tax. The fish he caught that day was worth enough to not only pay the Lord's tax but Peter's as well.

The blessing of those days of Heaven on earth spilled over to the nearby towns of Bethsaida (hometown of the Lord's first disciples, Peter and Andrew, James and John) and Chorazin. This tri-city area became the hub of the Lord's dealings in "Galilee of the Gentiles." These highly favored inhabitants heard the spoken Word coming from the living Word. They saw the visible glory of the invisible God. They tasted bread provided by the Bread from Heaven.

They, like the woman with the issue of blood at Capernaum, touched the Great High Priest who is touched with the feeling of our infirmity. Yet for all this they did not receive the One who had come to seek and save the lost. At last, He had to say: "Woe unto thee, Chorazin! woe unto thee, Bethsaida! for if the mighty works, which were done in you, had been done in Tyre and Sidon, they would have repented long ago in sackcloth and ashes…And thou, Capernaum, which art exalted unto heaven, shalt be brought down to hell" (Mt. 11:21-23). The place of untold blessing fell at last under the divine curse.

To the north of these cities, at the foot of mighty Mount Hermon, lies the ancient city of Laish, renamed Dan by the tribe of Dan when they chose this site (furthest from Jerusalem) instead of the land the Lord gave them near Joppa. They had been the first to institutionalize idolatry in Israel and this great rock face at present-day Banias, from which issues one of the main sources of the Jordan, was dedicated to idol worship. Here one of the golden calves was located in the days of King Jeroboam, the people pleaser. You can still see the niches in the rock that were used to house images. If ever there was a place under the curse of God, surely this would be it.

How symbolic, then that the Lord chose this as the backdrop for His earth-shaking announcement: "Upon this rock I will build My church" (Mt. 16:18). To the place of the cursed devil-worshippers came this magnificent revelation that God also has a Rock—the unshakable Christ. Upon this foundation would be erected the only structure that will survive the collapse of the universe. Indeed this whole world under the curse received in this announcement the hope of a blessing so wonderful that only God would have conceived it. Then the sacred writer adds, "From that time forth began Jesus to show unto His disciples, how that He must…suffer…and be killed." Ah, the true place of the curse and the blessing: "Christ…made a curse for us:…Cursed is every one that hangeth on a tree: that the blessing of Abraham might come on the Gentiles through Jesus Christ" (Gal. 3:13-14).

Ruins of the synagogue at Capernaum, our Lord's city after He left Nazareth. The synagogue is made of imported stone (notice the local black basalt stone in the foreground) and curiously is built facing away from Jerusalem.

Henry Van Dyke in the Hula Valley

All day we ride along the hills skirting the marshy plain of Huleh (or Hula). Here the springs and parent streams of Jordan are gathered, behind the mountains of Naphtali and at the foot of Hermon, as in a great green basin about the level of the ocean, for the long, swift rush down the sunken trench which leads to the deep, sterile bitterness of the Dead Sea. Was there ever a river that began so fair and ended in such waste and desolation?

Here in this broad, level, well-watered valley, along the borders of these vast beds of papyrus and rushes intersected by winding, hidden streams, Joshua and his fierce clans of fighting men met the Kings of the north with their horses and chariots, "at the waters of Merom," in the last great battle for the possession of the Promised Land. It was a furious conflict, the hordes of footmen against the squadrons of horsemen; but the shrewd command that came from Joshua decided it: "Hough their horses and burn their chariots with fire." The Canaanites and the Amorites and the Hittites and the Hivites were swept from the field, driven over the western mountains, and the Israelites held the Jordan from Jericho to Hermon (Josh. 11:1-15).

The springs that burst from the hills to the left of our path and run down to the sluggish channels of the marsh on our right are abundant and beautiful. Here is 'Ain Mellaha, a crystal pool a hundred yards wide, with wild mint and watercress growing around it, white and yellow lilies floating on its surface, and great fish showing themselves in the transparent open spaces among the weeds, where the water bubbles up from the bottom through dancing hillocks of clean, white sand and shining pebbles.

Here is 'Ain el-Belata, a copious stream breaking forth from the rocks beneath a spreading terebinth tree, and rippling down with merry rapids toward the jungle of rustling reeds and plumed papyrus. While luncheon is preparing in the shade of the terebinth, I wade into the brook and cast my fly along the ripples. A couple of ragged, laughing, bare-legged Bedouin boys follow close behind me, watching the new sport with wonder. The fish are here, as lively and gamesome as brook trout, plump, golden-sided fellows ten or twelve inches long. The feathered hooks tempt them, and they rise freely to the lure. My tattered pages are greatly excited, and make impromptu pouches in the breast of their robes, stuffing in the fish until they look quite fat. The catch is enough for a good supper for their whole family, and a dozen more for a delicious fish-salad at our camp that night. What kind of fish are they? I do not know: doubtless something scriptural and Oriental. But they taste good; and so far as there is any record, they are the first fish ever taken with the artificial fly in the sources of the Jordan.

The plain of Huleh is full of life. Flocks of waterfowl and solemn companies of storks circle over the swamps. The wet meadows are covered with herds of black buffaloes, wallowing in the ditches, or staring at us sullenly under their drooping horns. Little bunches of horses, and brood mares followed by their long-legged, awkward foals, gallop beside our cavalcade, whinnying and kicking up their heels in the joy of freedom. Flocks of black goats clamber up the rocky hillsides, following the goatherd who plays upon his rustic pipe quavering and fantastic music, softened by distance into a wild sweetness. Small black cattle with white faces march in long files across the pastures, or wander through the thickets of bulrushes and papyrus and giant fennel, appearing and disappearing as the screen of broad leaves and trembling plumes close behind them…

Along the higher ground are lines of black Bedouin tents, arranged in transitory villages. These flitting habitations of the nomads, who come down from the hills and lofty deserts to fatten their flocks and herds among unfailing pasturage, are all of one pattern. The low, flat roof of black goat's hair is lifted up by the sticks which support it, into half a dozen little peaks…Between these peaks the cloth sags down, and is made fast along the edges by intricate and confusing guy-ropes. The tent is…from twelve to thirty feet long, according to the wealth of the owner and the size of his family—two things which usually correspond.

—Henry Van Dyke in *Out-of-Doors in the Holy Land,* April 1908, pp. 267-271

The Sea of Galilee

*G*alilee, Tiberias, Gennesaret, Chinnereth—the lake has almost as many names as it has moods. The Sea of Galilee (from *galil*, "a harp") lies in northeastern Israel like a sparkling sapphire in the sun-drenched Jordan Valley. At almost 700 feet below sea level, it provides a moderated climate all year long. "The temper of the air is so well blended," wrote Josephus, "one may call this place the ambition of Nature…it is a happy contention of the seasons."

The lake is 13 miles long and 8 miles at its widest. It is fed partly by natural springs, but mostly by the waters of the upper Jordan. "Sweet water," wrote George Adam Smith, "full of fish, a surface of sparkling blue, tempting down breezes from above."

In fact, the lake has been swept by history as often as it is by the sudden storms that catch it unawares from the surrounding hills. It was with just such a surprise that the little villages on its shores received a Stranger who moved to Capernaum one day in the first century, A.D. But He would soon be a familiar sight, standing by the shore, riding in a boat, speaking to them on the hillside amphitheaters.

"Two thousand years ago, the Sea of Galilee was fringed with fertile plantations of palms, vineyards, olive groves, walnut and fig trees. The lakeside hummed with the the movement of fishermen and boat-builders," write Moshe Pearlman and Yaacov Yannai in their *Historical Sites in the Holy Land*. But as the centuries rolled by, the little inland sea was forgotten; the area lapsed into swamp and marsh. Then in 1909, the first cooperative farm, Kibbutz Degania, was founded and slowly the fruitfulness returned.

For years, explorers searched for the New Testament harbors along the water's edge. A few, like the harbor at Kursi on the eastern shore, were discovered by underwater survey in the early 1970's. But the history of Galilee's fishing centers laid under its lapping waves until the late 1980's when a dangerous drought caused the level of the lake to drop significantly and so expose a ring of ancient anchorages and harbors, 16 in all. Some of these are familiar names to the reader of the New Testament: Capernaum, Magdala, Bethsaida, and Gadara.

Capernaum (from *kfar nahum*, the village of Nahum), is referred to as the Lord's own city. It is the site of a large number of miracles performed by our Lord. Here occurred the draught of fishes (see Lk. 5:1-11) and Peter's catching of the lone fish with the tribute money in its mouth (see Mt. 17:24-27). Capernaum also saw the healing of a multitude of needy folk: two demoniacs (Mk. 1:21-28; Mt. 12:22-37); Peter's mother-in-law (Mt. 8:14-15); the centurion's servant (Mt. 8:5-13); a paralytic (Mk.

The northwest shore of the Sea of Galilee. On the horizon at center is the building built to commemorate the traditional site of the Sermon on the Mount. To the left is a large grassy outdoor "amphitheater" with exceptional accoustical properties.

2:1-12); the woman with an issue of blood (Mk. 5:25-34); Jairus' daughter (Lk. 8:40-56); two blind men (Mt. 9:27-31); and the man with a withered hand (Mt. 12:9-13).

Yet after all this, the people of Capernaum did not believe, and the One who had come to bless left them with a curse: "Woe unto you, Capernaum!" Two thousand years later, the town still lies in ruins. As you stand there on the northern shore of the lake, surrounded by the basalt remains of the city that once knew the gentle voice of heaven's lovely Man, you cannot help but feel something of the desolation of a soul without the Lord. But as you lift your eyes across the blue waves and up to the verdant hills, you also cannot help but remember that it was here that the Son of Man brought the only true hope to the human race. It was here that for our sakes He became poor that we might be rich.

It is a delightful exercise to take a walk along the Galilean shore at Tiberias on a summer evening. The sun will have long since disappeared behind the hills of the eastern Lower Galilee, but still the slopes of Gergesa and Gadara on the other side of the lake will be catching its lingering rays, turning them a pastel peach color. The water at our feet either laps against the promenade or gurgles its way back and forth through the pebbles along the shore. A refreshing breeze sweeps down from the hills and etches ever-changing patterns on the surface of the lake.

Fishermen, as they have for thousands of years, are preparing their little craft for a night of labor on the sea. They hope, before returning at dawn, to pull from its bosom a bountiful harvest, including an ample catch of *musht*, or St. Peter's fish, as it is called.

Laughter and chatter break the stillness and remind me that Tiberias is a town mostly of pleasure seekers. But so has it been since it was built by Herod Antipas just shortly before our Lord moved to Capernaum, across on the northern shore. Herod had built the city here to take advantage of the climate and of the hot mineral springs called Hammath (Hebrew for "hot") just south of the modern town. We never read of the Lord Jesus entering this city, though He ministered all about it.

Can you imagine Peter and John, Andrew and James, striding along this shore? See them mending their nets, sorting and salting their fish, these swarthy, sun-baked men who would become foundation stones in the Church. Think of Mary of Magdala and Matthew, the multitudes, the Master. They were all here. They all had seen the sun go down over the lake and watched its depths turn dark. But only One knew how dark it would get in the days that lay ahead. The darkness would become impenetrable at Golgotha, but, said the Saviour, "I will go before you into Galilee." So it was that after the sorrows of Calvary, the resurrected Christ made rendezvous with His own by the same shore from which He had first called them.

I will soon be climbing into my soft bed, a pillow under my head. Not so the One who had "nowhere to lay His head." Galilee will be hard for us to leave. There is something here that wraps itself around your soul. It must not have been easy either for the disciples to leave this lovely landscape for parts unknown, to bear the light of the gospel into the night of sin. They were used to working at night, it is true, but they would need the Master nearby as they did that night when they had caught nothing. It was good that they had His promise: "I am with you…"

I have watched the sea turn from pale blue to azure to emerald to inky black. I am dependent now on the light from the waterside cafés to make my way home. It is dark and chill; the wind is picking up. My friends who work in this land will tell you the same thing—it is dark here, and chill. And the wind is picking up. The storm warnings are out and the last great storm is rolling in. How thankful I am for those "lights along the shore" here, who go on shining for the despised Jesus in the very land He has loved and lost awhile.

I listen as the fishermen make their way out to sea, and remember the words of the Master who called a few men from this honest toil to follow Him. "I will make you fishers of men," He said. They left all and followed Him. The world has never been the same.

J

A. T. Schofield on Galilee

esus entered into a small sailing-boat in company with some other boats, probably going out to fish. Before they had gone very far, however, a great wind arose, and in an incredibly short space of time the roughness of the lake caused the waves to beat into the boat, so that it began to fill with water. Nowhere, perhaps, do these sudden squalls arise and subside so quickly as in Galilee.

We saw this in 1911 on coming down from Bethsaida-Julias to Capernaum (Tell-Hum). The lake was as a mirror and we had to row all the way, but the sky towards Magdala began to be overcast, and when we were re-embarking at Capernaum, after viewing the restored synagogue so marvelously rebuilt by the enterprise of the German Franciscan monks, the "father" urged us not to delay, but to hurry back to Tiberias, for a storm was about to descend upon the lake. Everything was so still and peaceful that I fear we paid but scant heed to his words; but, surely enough, we had hardly sailed a furlong with the light breeze which had sprung up when a squall burst upon us; the wind, rushing down from the horns of Hattin, came screaming over Magdala, and in less than five minutes we were surrounded with white waves and violently tossed upon the sea.

An easterly storm on Galilee (photo by Mendel Nun)

The wind increased rapidly in violence, and our Arab crew lost their heads and rushed about the boat, to our great danger, with loud cries of "Allah." They tried to furl the sail, but for a long time in vain; it kept escaping from their hands, and every moment we expected to see it torn from the mast. The waves were coming into the boat, and, as it was heavily laden, we were in no small fear for our lives.

At last, however, the canvas was wrapped round the mast, and our crew took to the oars; but even then it was with great difficulty we prevented the water from swamping us. Finally we reached Tiberias soaked to the skin, but far better able to understand this gospel story than we had ever been before.

It was a very similar storm that had occurred that day when Jesus was asleep in the hinder part of a ship, with His head on a pillow. He, however, was not consciously in the storm, for one who is asleep is elsewhere than in his surroundings. The disciples, almost frantic with fear, roughly woke their Master and brought Him into the stormy scene, crying, "Carest Thou not that we perish?"

Then, in a moment, the Creator who made the world and all that is therein, who holds the waters in the hollow of His hand, spake to His creatures, and the wind ceased, and there was a great calm. Familiar though they were with the presence of the Lord, the physical fears of the disciples were now succeeded by fear of another order, and they said one to another: "What manner of man is this that even the wind and the sea obey Him?"

—A. T. Schofield in *Where He Dwelt: Mind Pictures of Palestine*, dated 1914, pp. 172-174

The Golan: Place of Passage

The high tableland (1600-2300 feet above sea level) lying to the south of Mount Hermon was known in ancient times as Bashan. Its territory is also bounded by the Arabian Desert on the east, the Jordan Rift on the west, and the Yarmuk River on the south. Ruled by the giant king, Og, Bashan was taken from him at the battle of Edrei and given as part inheritance to Manasseh (Deut. 3:1-14). Once heavily forested, Bashan was as famous for its oak trees as Lebanon was noted for its cedars. The Phoenicians built their ships of fir from Hermon, their masts of cedar from Lebanon, and their oars of oak from Bashan (Ezek. 27:5-6).

Because of its rich fertility, the region was farmed extensively, and as the area was harvested of its trees, it became the "cowboy country" of Israel. The sleek bulls of Bashan raised here were highly prized. It is with some irony, then, that the ceremonially clean bulls are likened to the unclean roaring lions, as Jews and Gentiles, moving in for the kill, gathered around the exhausted Hind of the Morning (Ps. 22:12-13). It is no less ironic that a thriving kibbutz named *Aiyelet Hashahar* (Hind of the Morning) lies today at the foot of the Bashan cliffs in the beautiful Hula Valley.

But the ancient name of Bashan gave way to the Hebrew name of Golan, after the settlement in this region which was one of the six refuge cities provided by God for the inhabitants of the land (Deut. 4:41-43). Golan means *a place of passage*. It was located on the north side of the Yarmuk, 20 miles east of the Sea of Galilee. These refuge cities, three on each side of the Jordan River, were characterized by three essentials: altitude, accessibility, and availability. In elevated positions, they were like the city set on a hill of which the Saviour spoke; they could not be hid. They were also accessible—one in each region of the land. No one could be further than 30 miles from a place of refuge in Israel. As well, the cities were available—their gates were always open. One who had inadvertently shed blood could flee the kinsman-avenger to one of these cities. There at the gate, before the city fathers, the man-slayer would plead his case. If found not guilty of murder, he would make his home there until the death of the high priest.

The seventh, and perfect Refuge is opened to our guilty race in the New Testament when, in fulfillment of Isaiah's prophecy, a Man becomes a place of safety. He too is lifted up by the city gate for all to see. As accessible as a prayer, He waits the cry of the sinner, flushed with fear, fleeing from the wrath to come. There is help nowhere else, but there *is* help there. The Door is open; the refuge awaits not now the guiltless, but the guilty. And those who flee to Him are safe forever, for our High Priest will *never* die!

Because of the strategic importance of this plateau looming over the Galilee, the Golan has been the scene of some of the Middle East's most bloody fighting. The lines drawn by Britain and France in 1917 gave this territory to the Syrians. In 1948, on the declaration of the State of Israel, Syria began to fortify this natural containment. On June 5, 1967, the Six-Day War began with Egypt. By noon, the Jordanians were bombarding Jerusalem and the Syrians were shelling the kibbutzim in the north. Strikes by the Israeli Air Force against Egypt largely neutralized the southern threat. On Wednesday, the historic breakthrough at St. Stephen's Gate and Zion Gate gave the Jews access to the old city of Jerusalem, and set the Jordanian army in flight towards Amman. But the battle in the north was hard-won. A network of barbed-wire barricades and subterranean concrete bunkers linked with a honeycomb of innumerable tunnels produced bitter hand-to-hand combat. Not till Saturday did the road lie open to Damascus.

Again in 1973, the fiercest fighting took place here. With 1,400 tanks, the Syrian offensive reclaimed much of the land lost in 1967 before the Israelis were able to beat their way back, foot by foot, until they had taken even the summit of Hermon. They were twenty miles from Syria's capital.

But the greatest battle on the Heights was fought between the King of Light and one of the Prince of Darkness' lustiest generals. Here Saul of Tarsus lay in the dust, defeated by the One whom he sought to destroy. Here he yielded up his sword to be armed with the panoply of God (Acts 9; Eph. 6:10-18). Here he was recommissioned and sent forth to conquer men with the love of Christ. Who else but Jesus would take one of His chief enemies, save him, and place him in His own vanguard to share the victory?

Jezreel: the Swath

The word *swath* (or swathe) derives from the Old English *swaeth* for footstep. It is used to describe a row of cut grain left by a scythe or mowing machine, or for a space devastated by a scythe. Looking at a topographical map of Israel, the swath is obvious. On a northwest-southeast diagonal, the Y-shaped plain composed of a handful of valleys rises from the coast just north of the Carmel range, slashes its way through the central mountain spine, and merges with the Jordan Valley at the strategic city of Beth-shan.

This separating line between Galilee to the north and Samaria to the south has a score of names. The watershed at the midpoint in the plain is the site of the town of Jezreel, once the domain of Ahab and Jezebel. Here Elijah completed his eight-mile run ahead of the king's chariot. Here Jehu, after riding furiously from the land of Gilead east of the Jordan, slew Jezebel and Joram, and chased Joram's cousin from Jerusalem, King Ahaziah, across the plain to the south. He caught and executed him at Ibleam.

Thus, with Jezreel at its heart, the plain is often called by that name, or by its Greek equivalent, Esdraelon. These mean *may God sow*. Although Philip Schaff wrote in 1800, "It is now uninhabited, and only a small portion is cultivated," it was not always so. Isaiah called these the "fat valleys" (Isa. 28:1), and today this area forms the major portion of the breadbasket of Israel.

Imagine a fallen warrior, lying on his side. His feet lie at the edge of the Mediterranean. The Kishon River (where Elijah slew the prophets of Baal) would be his spine. The Carmel range (where the Battle of the Gods took place) is his quiver. His head rests in a large plain, enclosed by the Samaritan Hills. Mount Gilboa (where Saul and Jonathan died) would be the face protector, the Hill of Moreh (where Gideon routed the Midianites) his shield. The raised arm behind the shield follows the Harod River from the spring where Gideon's mighty men were chosen.

A fallen soldier is hardly an inappropriate symbol of the plain called by Napoleon "the cockpit of the world." When the strategic fortress of Megiddo (halfway along the southern flank) fell to the Egyptian forces of Thutmosis III, he wrote: "Capture it, and fortify it well; for to capture Megiddo is to capture a thousand towns." Along with these, the most illustrious conquerors in history have won or lost their laurels here—Sennacherib, Nebuchadnezzar, Alexander, Marc Antony. Allenby, the Ptolemies of Egypt, the Selucids, the Turks, the French and British, the Israeli Defense Forces have all fought here.

On the northern edge of the valley is Nazareth, home of the despised Galilean. He grew up in sight of the place where His triumph will at last be complete. Here God will not only sow but reap. Cutting a swath through our enemies, He will triumph gloriously! *Megiddo,* from the root *gawdad,* means to gather or to assemble by troops. History is witness that Armageddon has already lived up to its name. But the last great battle is still to come.

Seven gates provide access into the valley (see map). The western (and largest) entry is from the coastal plain where the road swings down from Tyre and Sidon (Jezebel's hometown and land of the great-hearted Syrophoenician). Today the modern port of Haifa sits at the mouth of the Kishon. But the strategic opening into Israel's heartland has been fortified through history. Here 80,000 Crusaders died in a two-year siege (1189-1191) by the Saracens, their last toehold in Palestine. Here Napoleon saw his hopes dashed to establish an eastern empire.

The northeastern gate (2), between Tabor and Moreh, opens into the Kisslot basin of the lower Galilee. This is a shorter route to points north and east, but due to its marshy condition in the rainy season, it could only be used part of the year. Here the Midianites fled in disarray from Gideon's 300 after the night surprise on Moreh. Here also Sisera was "discomfitted" and fled from Barak. When his chariot was mired in the sudden floodwaters of the Kishon, he fled on foot through either 2 or 3 on his flight back to Hazor. He never made it. Death came through the delicate hands of a woman and the unyielding point of a nail.

Gate 3 was the entrance of choice for those ascending the Jordan Valley and heading for Europe.

The road ran between Gilboa, where the shield of Saul was "vilely cast away," and the Philistine stronghold of Beth-shan where the decapitated bodies of the king and his sons were ignobly hung. The road continued past Shunem—home-away-from-home for Elisha—and Jezreel, where Ahab's palace stood. Through this passage rode the chariot of Jehu "furiously," where, by the purpose of God, judgment fell on the house of Ahab. Joram, Ahab's son now on the throne, was unceremoniously dispatched and cast on Naboth's vineyard to mingle his blood with the former owner of the land. Ahaziah, king of Judah, visiting his relatives in the north, fled from Jehu, making it as far as Ibleam (Gate 4) before he was caught and fatally wounded.

Through the south gate (4), heading to Egypt, came the Ishmaelite caravan that bought Joseph at Dothan, thus changing the course of history.

Gates 5-7 run through narrow passes cutting across the Carmel Range. Of these three, the central (6) is most strategic. It is the "back road" to Megiddo, used by Thutmosis III, Necho II, and Allenby to surprise the fortress at its northern end.

Most, if not all, of the armies slated to fight here in history's last great battle have *already* fought here. They have strategies established for this site in their manuals of war. Can you not imagine the king of the south, in an effort at surprise, coming through the Iron Pass (6) while the hordes from the east (the Moslems from Jordan to Indonesia?) enter by Gate 3? Syria (perhaps backed by Russia) would take the route from the Golan past the northwest shore of Galilee through Gate 2. Gate 1 would be the obvious entrance for the forces of the restored Roman Empire. That leaves Gates 4 and 5 for the forces of Antichrist being driven back from Jerusalem by Messiah Himself: *"And He gathered them together into a place called in the Hebrew tongue Armageddon."* However it unfolds, we know how the battle will end: *"The Lamb shall overcome them: for He is Lord of lords, and King of kings"* (Rev. 17:14).

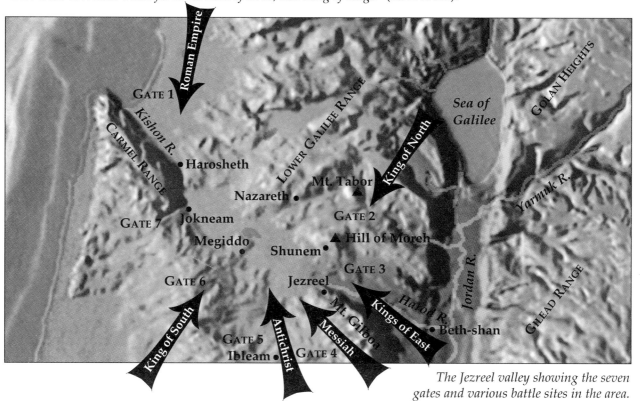

The Jezreel valley showing the seven gates and various battle sites in the area.

Photo: *The view from the Hill of Megiddo across the Valley of Jezreel (Armageddon).*
Inset: *A horse feeding trough (stone manger) at Megiddo, perhaps dating to the time of Solomon.*

The Classic Battlefield

*T*he main road (Route 75) through the heart of the Jezreel Valley heads for Nazareth or to Afula and Beth-shan. From Afula, another road reaches Nazareth in 15 minutes, but we choose instead Route 65, the Afula-Tiberias road. Upper Afula is built on the Hill of Moreh, site of the victory by "the sword of the Lord and of Gideon" over the Midianites. After having his troops thinned from 32,000 to 10,000 by simply asking the fearful to leave, Gideon's army was further decimated to a mere 300 by removing the unprepared at Ein Harod, the spring that still gurgles from the base of Mount Gilboa.

Interestingly, it was in this very grove of trees that Orde Wingate, a British officer, trained a handful of Jewish soldiers who became the backbone of the Israeli Defense Forces. He taught them that numbers don't matter, to use surprise, and that because they would never control the land numerically, they must hold it strategically. Ezer Weizman, founder of the Israeli Air Force, said that Wingate was more a missionary than a military man. His uniform was always wrinkled, and he thought little of rank, but he always had a Bible handy to point out the strategic significance of each location they visited.

Under cover of night, Gideon's 300 spread along the edge of the Midianite encampment, who had taken the high ground of Moreh. When, all of a sudden, the clay jars were smashed, the torches blazed, and the trumpets blasted in the still night air, the enemy was thrown into disarray. The sentries, no doubt seeing a division for every standard-bearer, called for a swift retreat.

A little further along the rim of Moreh on the right is an Arab village. This is Nain. Here, at the city gate one day, a crowd surrounding the bier of an only son met a crowd surrounding another only Son, the Life Himself. The funeral was interrupted and the young man restored to his mother.

Now looming ahead is a sugar-loaf mountain. One of the broken hills of the Lower Galilee Range, the dome-like Mount Tabor rises abruptly to 1,911 feet (588 m). In Old Testament days, it was the meeting point of the three tribal areas of Issachar, Zebulon, and Naphtali. But before we arrive at the base of Tabor, we see a road to the right that leads to a kibbutz called Ein Dor. Here the ill-fated Saul had supper with a witch the night before he fell on the slopes of Gilboa. The witch called up Samuel's familiar spirit because, said Saul, "I am sore distressed; for the Philistines make war against me, and God is departed from me, and answereth me no more." To the witch's horror, the Lord really sent Samuel back to deliver one postmortem message: "The Lord hath rent the kingdom out of thine hand," intoned the prophet.

The turnoff to Mount Tabor is on the left, but a word of warning: the climb is steep and narrow, with lots of hair-raising hairpins on the way to the summit. Our bus can't make it to the top, but a Nazareth company has the concession to take us in a fleet of stretch Mercedes taxis. It seems that, long ago, their blood was replaced by antifreeze. They chat merrily in broken English while the gravel dislodged by their spinning wheels cascades over the mountain edge. Some think I exaggerate until I tell them that on one trip we came across two men *hang-gliding* off the road. "They crazzzy!" remarked our driver, but at that moment I thought it a fairly sensible alternative to our present mode of travel. The rusting hulk of a car over one cliff did nothing to allay our concern.

What a panorama from the summit! There are two stunning views. One is to the south and west from the terrace of a Franciscan hospice. The other, to the north and east, must be approached carefully along the ruins of an earlier church building. We are reminded of the battle between Deborah and Barak's troops and the Canaanites under Sisera. It is obvious to us now that Sisera's armored division of 900 chariots of iron could never make the climb up this slope! Barak was safe there—but he could never be Israel's deliverer unless he came down in apparent weakness. Paul uses this as an illustration of the incarnation, crucifixion, resurrection, and exaltation of our Deliverer. First He must descend before He ascends. And when He ascended, "He led captivity captive, and gave gifts unto men." This is the Spirit's revision of Deborah and Barak's victory song. It was the conqueror's right to receive the spoils of the victory. But the One who subdued us when we were His enemies then enriched us with His triumphs and gave us back as gifts to the Church. Wonderful Deliverer!

Gilead: Israel's Pharmacy

With some reluctance, we turn our backs on the Jezreel Valley. There is still so much more here, but the remainder of the land beckons. We head east through what we earlier labeled Gate 3, the Harod River Valley, opening into the Jordan Valley at the Philistine stronghold of Beth-shan. We cross the Jordan at one of the more important of her more than 50 fords. This one, site of the slaughter by the Ephraimites of the Midianites fleeing Gideon's troops (Jud. 7:22), lies close by the confluence of the Jabbok River and the Jordan.

A road that followed the Wadi Fari'a through the Mountains of Ephraim crossed here and traversed the Jabbok valley up into the heartland of Gilead. This road linked Samaria and Gilead, providing an alternative "back door" route to and from the Vale of Shechem.

Of course, this was not the way that Israel arrived in their conquest of Trans-Jordan. The region "on the other side Jordan" was occupied by Amorite, Ammonite, Moabite, and Edomite kingdoms. The Amorite kingdoms of Og (occupying Golan) and Sihon (in Gilead) were destroyed when they resisted Moses' request for peaceful passage through their land. The three kingdoms to the south—Ammon, Moab, and Edom, were left alone because they were related to Israel through Esau and Lot's two sons.

The Gilead dome is covered with rolling wheatlands, orchards, and forests. It stretches from the Yarmuk cliffs to some point north of the Dead Sea, a line that moved with the ebb and flow of history. Rising to an elevation of more than 3,000 feet, it has the highest rainfall in Trans-Jordan south of the Galilee (28") because the Jezreel Valley gives an opening to rain-laden clouds from the Mediterranean. This combination of warmth and precipitation provided ideal conditions for growing the aromatic spices and medicinal herbs for which the region became renowned. Jeremiah, in seeking some relief for his pain over Israel's sins, cries: "Is there no balm in Gilead; is there no physician there?" (Jer. 8:22). Later, he anticipates the day when the Lord will avenge Himself of His enemies. Then Egypt, Ethiopia, and Libya will find nothing to relieve their agony: "In vain shalt thou use many medicines" (Jer. 46:11).

In Numbers 32, Gad was granted central Gilead. In this way the terms Gad and Gilead became almost synonymous. However, many from Ephraim across Jordan also settled there in sufficient numbers to have the area renamed "the forest of Ephraim" (cf. 2 Sam. 18:6).

Gilead is richly woven through the tapestry of Israel's history. It first appears when angry Laban (following a 400-mile race!) caught Jacob after his stealthy departure from Paddan-Aram (Gen. 31). Through a warning word from the Lord, Laban and Jacob made a covenant and commemorated it with a heap of stones set up as a pillar. This is the meaning of Gilead—a heap of testimony.

We will consider more of the people and events in the hills of Gilead, but for now let us linger by the banks of the Jabbok, just outside the town of Penuel. Night falls. Jacob has sent his family and possessions on ahead. He is left alone. I cannot do better for you than to quote a classic section from Sir George Adam Smith's *Historical Geography:*

"One has seen the Jabbok from one's childhood—the midnight passage of a ford, the brief section of a river gleaming under torches, splashed and plowed by struggling animals, cries of women and children above the noise; and then left alone, with the night, the man, and the river: the wrestle with God beside the struggling stream, and the dawn breaking down the valley on a changed life . . .

"The highest fame of Jabbok will be its first fame, and not all the sunshine, or ripening harvests along its live length, can be so bright as that first gleaming and splashing of its waters at midnight, or the gray dawn breaking on Israel next morning. This history of Gilead is a history of material war and struggle, civilization enduring only by perpetual strife. But by the Jabbok its first hero was taught how man has to reckon in life with God also, and that his noblest struggles are in the darkness, with the Unseen."

Oh, the wonder of it, when God puts Himself into the hands of a man, as He does each time we pray or worship or serve Him! The blessing comes when we can no longer wrestle with Him—when we can only cling. And it always happens at Peniel, where we see "the face of God."

Beyond the Jordan

Having crossed into Transjordan ("beyond the Jordan") to tour the Gilead range in our previous visit, we will head south into the high tableland of Moab. In fact, the borders between Gilead, Ammon, Moab, and Edom shifted north and south over the centuries like the tides, depending on the relative power of these kingdoms.

Much like the frontiers of past generations—the "wild West," or the Yukon, the rugged eastern plateau attracted personalities that matched its terrain. Individualists, desperados, fugitives from justice and men longing for open spaces found their way across the Jordan into the "wild East."

Here Jacob, still fearing his brother's wrath, instead of following him on the lonely, uninhabited road south to mount Seir (ideal for an ambush), turned west along the valley of the Jabbok to Succoth where he built a house and a refuge for his cattle. Then, crossing the Jordan, he traversed the western heights and no doubt breathed a sigh of relief as he "came in peace" to Shechem.

But he would not be the last "man on the run" who would find refuge in these forlorn limestone folds. Across their craggy face in abject terror raced the remainder of the Midianite army, hotly pursued by Gideon and his men. When the elders of Succoth and Penuel refused help to Gideon's troops who were "faint, yet pursuing," he in rough humor "taught the men of Succoth" a lesson with the aid of the wilderness thorns.

Can you not envision the "wild East" posse of Jair with his thirty sons descending in a cloud of dust upon some errant rancher to execute frontier justice? For 22 years he thus "judged Israel."

After the death of Jair, in the sad litany of the book of Judges, the Israelites once again forsook the Lord and served the very gods of the nations from which the Lord had delivered them! When Ammon (whose land was squeezed between Gilead and Moab) crossed the Jordan to fight against Israel, Israel cried to the Lord for help.

"Go and cry unto the gods which you have chosen; let them deliver you..." said the Lord.

Israel said, "We have sinned," and put away the strange gods, but had they really learned their lesson? The Lord reinforced it with an illustration close to home. Looking about for a deliverer, the men of Gilead asked Jephthah, "a mighty man of valor," if he would lead them to victory. But Jephthah, an illegitimate son, had been scorned and rejected by polite society in favor of his brothers.

"Did ye not hate me, and expel me out of my father's house?" he asked. "Why are ye come unto me now when ye are in distress?" How ironic! In the hard times, Israel came to God (and His deliverer, Jephthah); in the easy times, they turned their backs on divine help and sought their idols (and Jephthah's brothers). Do we each feel a twinge at our hearts when we read this?

What shall we say of the inhabitants of Jabesh-Gilead, world-borderers who "came not up to Mizpeh to the Lord"? After a great slaughter, their daughters were given as wives to the men of Benjamin. Later, Saul of Benjamin, in his first victory, delivered the city from Nahash (*the serpent*).

Elijah, rugged prophet from these rugged hills, hid here somewhere from the wrath of Ahab. And David, who had brought these lands under Israel's control, fled to Mahanaim when hounded by Absalom. Here, too, he wept out his lament for the wayward prince he had loved and lost.

To the south lie the imposing mountains of Moab. In the morning hours they come to life slowly, rosy red, then peach and lilac. But in the evening, the Moab range is first drenched in scarlet and then hangs like a purple curtain along the eastern rim of the Dead Sea. At the north end of the sea, 27 miles south of Amman, is Nebo (meaning *height*), the highest point of the ridge called Pisgah in the Abarim range. Here Israel's deliverer looked for the last time on the encampment and beyond to the Land of Promise. There he had "high honor" and "God's own hand in that lonely land to lay him in the grave."

From this land under the curse of the Moabite—this land of wily Balak and his rent-a-prophet, Balaam, ponderous Eglon, and rebellious Mesha—comes the lovely figure of Ruth, guileless, gracious, gentle, to put her trust in the God of Israel and to find herself in the very lineage of the Messiah Himself!

Who is This from Edom?

Wadi Hasa (the biblical Brook Zered—Deut. 2:13) carries precipitation off the Transjordan Range, flowing west-northwest into the south end of the Dead Sea near Zoar. This wadi (seasonal river) formed the natural boundary between the land occupied by the two illegitimate sons of Lot—Moab and Ammon (on the north), and the children of the man with no appetite for spiritual things—Esau (to the south). This land of Edom followed the range often called Mount Seir ("the hairy one" probably because of the scrub forests there), continuing southward from the Zered all the way to the Red Sea at the ancient port of Ezion-Geber, where Solomon floated his navy.

The territory is rugged indeed. These mountains (reaching elevations of 4500 ft.) parallel the Arabah, the desert-like portion of the Rift Valley that swings down toward the heart of Africa. Along the western crest, there is sufficient rainfall to grow wheat and barley. Much of the landscape is limestone and chalk, but the steep western slope is Nubian sandstone, making the name Edom ("red") appropriate.

A key thoroughfare, the King's Highway (now called the Mountain Road) was a well used trade route through Edom during the whole biblical period. It extended from Damascus to the Red Sea near modern day Elat and Aqaba. But Edom refused passage to their "brother," the travel-weary Israelites (Num. 20:14-21), requiring a long detour through the sweltering Eastern Arabian Desert. But first they stopped at Mount Hor, thought by some to be Jebel Harun, rising 4,780 feet about two miles west of Petra. Others fix the site at Jebel Madra, northwest of Kadesh-Barnea (Ain Qadeis). Here Aaron was stripped of his high priestly garments and ascended to his own funeral. Could any of us lift our eyes to the heights of Hor without lifting our hearts to the heights of heaven to thank God for that Great High Priest "who ever liveth to make intercession for us"?

The King's Highway obviously provided endless possibilities for robbers. The Edomites, who replaced the Horites (Gen. 14:6; 36:20-21, 29-30), were also replaced circa 300 B.C. by the Nabateans from North Africa (although Edomites, like the Herods, continued to have influence in the area). At first, the Nabateans plundered caravans going between Arabia, Syria, and Egypt, but soon found it better business to exact tolls instead. They flourished until crushed by the Romans in 106 A.D. at the battle for Petra.

The Nabateans prospered, extending their kingdom all the way to Damascus (Aretas, king over Damascus when Paul was converted there, was a Nabatean—2 Cor. 11:32). They made their capital at the breathtaking rose-red city of Petra (also called Sela and Joktheel). The natural fortress had been inhabited from antiquity. Amaziah captured it after defeating Edom in the valley of salt (2 Ki. 14:7-8). But the Nabateans beautified the city, situated 50 miles south of the Dead Sea.

The Romans also carved homes, baths, palaces, and a 4,000 seat amphitheater into the blood-red rock. As many as 7,000 inhabitants lived there during that time. But the Romans were followed by the Byzantines, the Crusaders, and the Moslems. Then Petra was lost to the world until 1812, when a determined Johann Burckhardt, posing as a Moslem, stood overwhelmed as he looked into the valley.

Some suggest the last chapter there has not yet been written. Perhaps the little Jewish remnant during the Time of Jacob's Trouble will take refuge in its rocky folds. That would explain this haunting reference: "Who is this that cometh from Edom, with dyed garments from Bozrah (another fortress nearby)? …travelling in the greatness of His strength?" The answer does not linger: "I that speak in righteousness, mighty to save." Another question: "Wherefore art Thou red in Thine apparel…?" "I have trodden the winepress alone…For the day of vengeance is in Mine heart, and the year of My redeemed is come. And I looked, and there was none to help…therefore Mine own arm brought salvation" (Isa. 63:1-5).

It has been a favorite path of escape to head east across the Jordan. And wouldn't it be just like the Lord to lead His people Israel in triumph through the very territory they were forbidden to traverse when they first came to take possession of the land? Is that not what He will do with us? The region where we have fought and often faltered, "the heavenlies" of Ephesians 6:12, will also be the place of our final triumph when our Deliverer leads us in victory right through enemy territory and up to glory.

The Hill Country of Samaria

Old Jacob had learned a thing or two in life. There had been more than a few twists and turns in the road since he fled from the wrath of his twin. That first day's run had been up hill and down dale for more than 50 miles. At last, with the sun extinguished in the Great Sea, the scion of the house of Abraham lay down for a fitful sleep, so exhausted that a stone could make do as a pillow. It was a night he would never forget. There at Bethel he had his first real dealings with the Lord, seeing the link with heaven that Christ said was none other than Himself in John 1:51.

Now down in Egypt, with the deep shadows of death cast across his pathway again, the old patriarch brought the blessing of God down on the heads of his sons. Jacob would not wrest the bloodline by giving Joseph the honor of the firstborn. That would go to Judah, lineage of Messiah. However Jacob adopted Joseph's two sons, Ephraim and Manasseh, and by giving them one portion each, he effectively gave Joseph the equivalent of the firstborn's double blessing. Love found a way. (See the double blessing of the "Church of the firstborn" in Romans 8:17—"heirs of God, and joint-heirs with Christ.")

How appropriate, then, that the land given to Joseph's boys included Bethel, the place where their grandfather found rest, revelation and, 20 years later, restoration (Gen. 35:1-15). The hill country of Samaria was Jacob's gift to his favored son. It was this very territory that Joseph had traversed as he looked for his brothers. His father was living near Hebron and Jacob's shepherd-sons had meandered north from there as the summer heat had parched the southern grasslands. Joseph had been directed to Shechem, an 80-mile walk, but his brothers were not there. They were, a passerby informed him, at Dothan, 20 miles further. But as we know, Joseph's journey had only just begun. From Canaan to Egypt, from prison to palace, and then to make the long trek back, Joseph's bones wandered with Israel forty years until they were buried, probably at Shechem where he had come seeking his brothers at the first.

Samaria's northern boundary is easy to trace along the southern edge of the Jezreel Valley. But her southern border is as difficult to map as it was to defend. With the ebb and flow of military dominance between Judah and Samaria, the line moved north and south. When first divided in the days of Jeroboam and Rehoboam, the line ran just south of Bethel. But Baasha pushed his outposts as far south as Ramah, only four miles north of Jerusalem. Much later, in the inter-Testament period, the Maccabees carried the frontier as far north as the Wadi Ishar near Shiloh. That would make the distance through Samaria north on the Patriarch's Highway no more than a good day's walk. But few self-respecting Jews would risk contamination by passing through this territory. With what force, then, did the artless words fall on John's New Testament readers concerning our Lord: "He must needs go through Samaria" (Jn. 4:4).

The whole area is named after the mountain of Shemer, which rises as a solitary hill commanding the valley through which the road travels that links the coast with the mountain road north and south. Once properly fortified, it was almost impregnable. It took Sargon three years to capture it (2 Ki. 17:5). Here ruled the wicked Ahab and Jezebel. Here ministered Elijah and Elisha. Here God delivered the city and used four beggars sitting outside the city wall to bring the good news to the inhabitants (2 Ki. 7).

The highway heads south from here, then twists east to pass through the vale of Shechem between mounts Ebal and Gerizim. Here Jacobs two boys, Simeon and Levi, took matters into their own hands, Jacob-like, and made Jacob's new name, Israel, to "stink among the inhabitants" (Gen. 34:30). Something had to be done, but Israel, God's prince, was learning to let God handle such problems in His own way.

Twelve miles south of Shechem lies the old village of Seilun, the site of ancient Shiloh. It is a gray mound, quite isolated even today, as it was in the days when Israel gathered to celebrate the "feasts of Jehovah" here for 400 years. It was here that news arrived from heaven one night that judgment would begin at the house of God; the boy Samuel would become a transitional ruler in Israel until God would establish His king in Jerusalem. That too would fail, and eventually Israel would crucify their King outside the city gates. But that would not be the last chapter. It will not be written "until Shiloh come," said Jacob, "and unto Him shall the gathering of the people be" (Gen. 49:10).

The location of Shiloh in central Samaria (the double inheritance of Joseph through his sons, Ephraim and Manasseh). Here the tabernacle was pitched from the conquest under Joshua until the ark of the covenant was captured by the Philistines in the days of Eli. Here the boy Samuel heard the voice of God, answering, "Speak, Lord, Thy servant heareth."

McCheyne & Bonar at Samaria's Hill

Our route now lay northwest over a considerable ridge, during the ascent of which we obtained a view of many distant villages; and among others Ramla, on an eminence. When we had gained the summit, the hill of Samaria came in sight, rising out of the plain to the height of about four hundred feet. It is an oblong hill sloping up toward the west, and has a considerable extent of tableland on the top. The plain, near the head of which it stands, stretches far to the west, and the mountains that enclose it are lofty. It is a hill in the midst of higher hills; a noble situation for a royal city. A grove of olives covers the plain, and the lower part of the southern side of the hill...

We read over the prophecy of Micah regarding Samaria as we drew near to it, and conversed together as to its full meaning. We asked Dr. Keith what he understood by the expression, "I will make Samaria *as an heap of the field.*" He replied, that he supposed the ancient stones of Samaria would be found, not in the form of a ruin, but gathered into heaps in the same manner as in cleaning a vineyard, or as farmers at home clear their fields by gathering the stones together...we found the conjecture to be completely verified. We halted at the eastern end of the hill beside an old aqueduct, and immediately under the ruin of an old Greek church which rises on this side above the miserable village of Sebaste (Herod rebuilt the city and called it Sebaste, which means "august, or venerable," in honor of Augustus Caesar; but God had written its doom centuries before)...

We ascended on foot by a narrow and steep pathway, which soon divides into two, and conducts past the foundations of the ruined church to the village. The pathway is enclosed by rude dikes, the stones of which are large and many of them carved, and these are piled rather than built upon one another. Some of them are loose and ready to fall. Many are peculiarly large, and have evidently belonged to ancient edifices. Indeed, the whole face of this part of the hill suggests the idea that the buildings of the ancient city had been thrown down from the brow of the hill.

Ascending to the top, we went round the whole summit, and found marks of the same process everywhere. The people of the country, in order to make room for their fields and gardens have swept off the old houses, and poured the stones down into the valley. Masses of stone, and in one place two broken columns, are seen, as it were, on their way to the bottom of the hill. In the southern valley, we counted thirteen large heaps, most of them piled up round the trunks of the olive trees. The church above mentioned is the only solid ruin that now remains where the proud city once stood. In the houses of the villagers, we saw many pieces of ancient columns, often laid horizontally in the wall; in one place, a Corinthian capital, and in another, a finely carved stone. Near the village, and in the midst of a cultivated field, stood six columns, bare and without their capitals, then seven more that appear to have formed the opposite side of the colonnade...

These are all that remain of Samaria, "the crown of pride." The greater part of the top of the hill is used as a field; the crop had been reaped, and the villagers were busy at the thrashing-floor. Part of the southern side is thickly planted with figs, olives, and pomegranates. We found a solitary vine, the only representative of the luxuriant vineyards which once supplied the capital. At one point, a fox sprang across our path into the gardens, a living witness of an unpeopled city.

It was most affecting to look round this scene of desolation, and to remember that this was the place where wicked Ahab built his house of Baal, where cruel Jezebel ruled, and where Elijah and Elisha did their wonders. But above all, it filled the mind with solemn awe to read over on the spot the words of God's prophet uttered 2500 years before: "I will make Samaria as an heap of the field, and as plantings of a vineyard; and I will pour down the stones thereof into the valley, and I will discover the foundations thereof."

—Andrew Bonar and Robert Murray McCheyne in *A Mission of Inquiry to the Jews from the Church of Scotland in 1839,* pp. 218-220

Who Are the Samaritans?

There are still Samaritans in the land of Israel. Huddled together in small communities in old Jaffa and in the shadow of their ancient place of worship, Mount Gerizim, they keep largely to themselves. Nablus (corrupted from "Neapolis" meaning new city) is the present name for Shechem, the focus of their community. It lies some 40 miles north of Jerusalem in a confined valley between Mount Ebal to the north (elevation, 3,000 feet) and the lesser Gerizim on the south (150 feet lower). At some point their bases are only a few hundred yards apart. The majority of the domed-roof, lattice-windowed houses have been made from the soft, white limestone of Mount Ebal, but the settlement has crept up the other mountain slope where numerous and copious springs emerge.

In Old Testament times this provided the ideal location for a kind of national amphitheater. Here Joshua gathered Israel midway in the conquest of Canaan (between the taking of Ai-Bethel and the victory over the southern confederacy in the valley of Aijalon). Six tribes ascended one mountain, six climbed the other; the priests and Levites stood with the Ark of the Covenant in the valley below. Then, in fulfillment of Moses' instructions (Deut. 27 & 28), as each curse was read out by Joshua, the million voices from Ebal thundered into the valley, "Amen!" Then as each blessing was given, a million voices from Gerizim answered, "Amen!" Thus it has ever been: if you obey the Lord you will be blessed; if you disobey, you fall under the curse.

But wait! Joshua wasn't finished. Watch as he climbs one of the mountains to build an altar made of uncut stones to the Lord. On it were offered burnt (acceptance) offerings and peace (reconciliation) sacrifices. Which mountain was it? Gerizim, the mount of blessing? No, it was erected on Ebal, mount of the curse, because it is then, when guilty of disobedience, that we need the sacrifice. The New Testament Joshua, our Lord Himself, ascended another mount of cursing and provided an acceptable sacrifice for every repentant lawbreaker. That day His own nation cried, "Crucify! Crucify!" because they wanted Him under the curse of God. But by the happiest of circumstances, God wanted Him under the curse as well. "Christ hath redeemed us from the curse of the law, being made a curse for us: for it is written, Cursed is every one that hangeth on a tree" (Gal. 3:13).

The name "Samaritan" comes from the name of the central province of ancient Israel. This in turn was derived from the capital city of the northern kingdom, established by Omri, sixth king of Israel, in the ninth century BC. As mentioned earlier, he had named it after its original owner, Shemer.

However, the derivation of the people is more difficult to ascertain than that of their name. The Samaritans themselves maintain that they are the remnant of the tribe of Ephraim and that the split with the Jews came over the incompetence of Eli's sons. An alternate view dates the schism to the time of the return of the Jews from Babylon. The Samaritans were those who remained in Israel throughout the captivity and intermarried with their Assyrian captors. They were rejected by the Jewish populace as being defiled and therefore having no place in Jerusalem. They established their own worship center on the slopes of Gerizim where to this day they meet, offering animal sacrifices on their holy days.

This territory is rife with biblical importance. Just take a look around you. See Abram driving in his tent pegs for the first time in Canaan (Gen. 12:6). Watch Jacob as he digs a well here, a well upon whose wall the Saviour Himself would sit. Joseph was deeded land here by his father (Jn. 4:5-6). Joshua gathered the nation onto these slopes again at the end of his life to give his farewell message: "Choose you this day whom ye will serve…" (Josh. 24). And hundreds of years later Israel did choose—this time between Rehoboam and Jeroboam—at the same natural outdoor meeting place (1 Ki. 12).

The New Testament relates three fascinating stories regarding Samaritans. There is the story of one who turned around, one who turned aside, and one who turned back. They have rich lessons for us today. The incident of the woman at the well (Jn. 4) is great instruction on witnessing for God; the "good Samaritan" is a lesson on working for God (Lk. 10); the Samaritan leper, one of ten, can teach us about worshiping God (Lk. 17:16).

A present-day Samaritan elder

The tale of the Samaritan woman begins with the statement that Jesus "must needs go through Samaria." It was not the way any self-respecting Jew would travel, but the Saviour had a rendezvous that day. And the Spirit makes a point of associating the scene of the meeting with Jacob and Joseph. Could it be to remind us of the blessing of Joseph by Jacob in Genesis 49? "Joseph is...a fruitful bough by a well; whose branches run over the wall" (v. 22). Here the True Vine has His branches run over the wall of Judaism so that a sin-weary woman might pluck His sweet fruit. Tasting, she finds that the Lord is good, and happy is the person who trusts in Him (see Ps. 34:8).

The Lord Jesus begins with something she knows: He talks about water and the well. He then talks about something she doesn't want Him to know: her sinful life. Then, and only then, He introduces what she doesn't know but now has a thirst to know: how to have a drink of living water that can quench the longings of the soul. The dear woman, having tasted it herself, returned to the village with a desire to make others thirsty. And she did, with the provocative statement: "Come, see a Man that told me all things that ever I did. It couldn't be the Messiah, could it?" Soon a stream of townsfolk could be seen wending their way to the Source, having tasted the water from the river that flowed from within their transformed neighbor in fulfillment of the Saviour's promise (Jn. 4:14).

The parable of the Good Samaritan was occasioned by the question of a lawyer. Seeking to justify his self-centered lifestyle, he was intent on limiting the force of the command to love our neighbor as ourselves. "Who is my neighbor?" he queried.

In response, the Lord told a story as current as the morning paper. A violent crime—popularly referred to as a mugging—had occurred and the victim lay wounded by the roadside. But what roadside? Did the Lord arbitrarily select the road from Jerusalem to Jericho? I hardly think so. It is the very road traveled by Jews wishing to avoid Samaria en route to Galilee! Yet here is a Samaritan, with his first-aid kit—bandages and medicine—looking for people to help. That is the spirit of neighborliness, the spirit that brought the Saviour from heaven's heights to our little planet. When we did not seek Him or love Him, He came to meet our need. It is a lesson which should not be lost on us in this needy world.

The third Samaritan story tells of ten lepers brought together by the sad, strange fellowship of need. In this case at least, Jews had dealings with a Samaritan, for one of them—already an outcast from Jewish society—had become an outcast from his own people as well when he contracted the dreaded disease. But the Saviour came and met them in their need, healing them with a word. With unbridled joy, the nine Jewish members of the little band began making plans for their religious ceremonies at the temple and their reentry into society. The Samaritan had no place in their festivities. He was as unwelcome in Jerusalem as the blessed Man who healed him. Falling at the feet of the Lord Jesus, he worshiped Him.

There is, no doubt, a place for activity in the things of God. It is important to obey the Word. But the haunting question flies to our hearts from the Master's lips: "Where are the nine?" Only one returned to give the Lord the praise He was due. Am I like the Samaritan in this?

May these three lessons from a despised people grip our souls today. May God help us to make others thirsty for Christ. May He give us eyes to see and hearts to seek our needy neighbors. But in all our busyness for Him, may we not miss the opportunities to fall at His feet in thankfulness and worship.

Photo: *The ruins of one of the main gates into the fortified Samaria, capital of the ten tribes after the division of the nation in the days of Rehoboam, Solomon's son. The city was enlarged and beautified extensively during the reign of Ahab, including his fabled ivory palace.*

Map: *The land of Samaria stretched from the coast to the Jordan River and from Judea to Galilee, producing a barrier to travel for orthodox Jews who had "no dealings" with the Samaritans. Hence there was no reason that Jesus "must needs go through Samaria" except that He had a divine appointment with the woman at the well.*

W

e arrive at Nablous, the ancient Shechem, a few hours before sunset, on the eve of the Passover; and, in company with other visitors we begin to climb Mount Gerizim by a rough track leading from the back of the town. Reaching the summit after a strenuous climb, we find a mixed crowd already assembled at the ceremonial site—Samaritans, Moslems, Jews, some Palestine darmes, a few outside visitors and a number of Government officials. The plateau, where the Passover is to be celebrated, is about 3000 ft. above sea level.

Tonight there will be observed on this mountain, saturated as it is with Bible history, a feast absolutely unique both for its antique origin and its deep Scriptural interest. So long as the Temple Area in Jerusalem remains in Moslem hands, the Jews throughout the world are without a lawful place for the offering of sacrifice. Hence this annual celebration of the Passover by a remnant of the ancient Samaritan people excites a good deal of interest amongst the Jewish community.

As the sun begins to settle in the west, everything is in readiness for the coming ceremony. In a newly-dug trench we see a number of big cauldrons bubbling over a brushwood fire like so many geysers. Near at hand, and dug also in the ground is an improvised well-shaped oven, about nine feet deep. It is being heated to redness by blazing thorn-bushes and pieces of wood. Not far away are the rows of Samaritan tents pitched for this occasion.

The actual proceedings of the Passover begin when twelve venerable elders, dressed in white robes and with white turbans emerge from the tents and pass solemnly through the crowd to the center of the gathering. With upturned palms and faces, they kneel on mats facing the site upon which once stood the ancient Samaritan Temple. The most conspicuous member of the group is the patriarchal figure of the high priest. He kneels at the head of the group, and again and again his eyes glance towards the setting sun as he continues to chant from the twelfth chapter of the Book of Exodus: "And this day shall be unto you for a memorial; and ye shall keep it a feast to the Lord throughout your generations; ye shall keep it a feast by an ordinance for ever."

As the crucial moment of sunset draws near, all eyes seem riveted on this venerable old man. The handsome face, with its distinct Semitic cast, the snowy-beard and flowing white robes present a striking picture. It is hard to convince the mind that one is not looking at some make-believe piece of acting, instead of a genuine and historic relic of Bible days. As a matter of fact, it is a bit of the world's most ancient regime projected into this twentieth century; and the setting of the scene is as genuine as the performance itself.

Quite unconscious of the vital role they must presently assume in the program, a small flock of lambs moves about in complete liberty, nibbling here and there at the scanty herbage—the last bite—for the knife and the fire are close upon them. The embodiment of gentle innocence, they are, nonetheless, the victims chosen for the Passover, and they seem to captivate our thought and attention. "In the tenth day of this month they shall take to them every man a lamb, according to the house of their fathers, a lamb for a house."

Suddenly there is a movement among the crowd, followed by a tenseness as though something great is about to happen. Some youths, dressed in white linen, probably the firstborn of the Samaritan families, advance from the congregation, and each seizes a lamb from the flock. The firstborn and the victim are now clearly identified.

Just as the sun dips down in splendor beneath the distant waters of the Mediterranean, the high priest utters a final blessing; and as the last word dies away, the fathers of the Samaritan households step forward, knives in hand. "And the whole assembly of the congregation of Israel shall kill it in the evening" (Ex. 12:6). Knives are unsheathed; there is a sudden glint of steel, and, the next moment, all the lambs are struggling in death. The application of boiling water makes the removal of the fleeces a simple matter, after which each carcass is dressed with ceremonial nicety. The offal and inedible parts are

A Passover ceremony on the summit of Mount Gerizim

removed for burning, care being taken that no bone of the victim is broken. After being salted, the carcasses are lowered into the heated oven, the mouth of which is covered and finally sealed with clay.

The sprinkling of the blood of the victims upon the door of each tent ends the first part of the ceremony. The chanting ceases. The priests in white linen seem to fade away in the darkness like phantoms, as they silently withdraw to their tents to await the hour of midnight. The visitor now feels as though he has been deserted, and realizes, for the first time, that he has really no part nor lot in this unique gathering. So he must just sit around the smoldering fires on the chilly mountain top, and try to while away the hours between now and the Passover Feast at midnight.

The memory of this waiting time spent on Gerizim lives still vividly in my mind. I see again the smoldering fires, the ghostly tents, the stars twinkling down upon the scene, just as others must have seen them throughout millenniums. But, from the brink of Jacob's Well, somewhere down there in the darkness, the words of the Samaritan woman seem wafted upward to my ears: "Our fathers worshiped in this mountain," and the Lord's reply, "They that worship Him, must worship Him in spirit and in truth" (Jn. 4:24). Somehow I felt that both "Spirit" and "Truth" were the two absent guests from the Passover on Gerizim that night. One could not but think of that lonely garden in the city of Jerusalem on the night of the world's great and final Passover, when under a tree in Gethsemane, the Lamb of God once wrestled all alone, sweating, as it were, "great drops of blood falling down to the ground." There was but one genuine link between Golgotha and what we had witnessed this night on Gerizim—the shedding of blood and the death of the innocent victim. Even so, the contrast was one of infinitude. With the one there was blank ignorance and a consequent indifference to approaching death; with Him, the foreknowledge and the anguish of His self-appointed sacrifice, yet withal the love that prompted Him to drain the bitter cup—for me. "For this cause came I into the world." In the face of Golgotha, Gerizim was obsolete: "For even Christ, our Passover, is sacrificed for us" (1 Cor. 5:7), and "there remaineth no more sacrifice for sins." So this Samaritan sacrifice was nineteen centuries too late, and the sacrificial blood had been shed once more in vain; yet not, perhaps, entirely in vain, seeing that the vast difference between the shadow of the Passover and the tremendous reality of the Crucifixion had been brought home to the mind in so vivid a manner.

I spent a part of the remaining chilly hours inside the tent of the high priest's son and heir. He had kindly invited me inside for a friendly chat. We talked of many things—the history of the Samaritans, the rival claims of Mount Moriah and Mount Gerizim, an age-long argument which still drags on…

The subject then drifted round to the Passover and its meaning. Careful questioning failed to elicit any intelligent apprehension in the minds of these people as to the real reason for the shedding of blood, the death of the lamb in place of the first-born, and the approach to God with empty hands during this ceremony of the Passover, as well as the sprinkling of the blood upon the doors of the tents. To them it was but a venerable and historic formality, a joyful feast, and a memorial of past deliverance on that fateful night in Egypt. The vast plan and purpose of God's redemptive work, as revealed in the person of Christ, the true Passover Lamb, did not seem to have ever crossed their minds.

As with the Jews, so with the Samaritans, and as, we must sorrowfully admit, with millions in Christendom, the shadows of ritual and formality had completely obsessed the mind, to the entire exclusion of substance and reality. Truly, "the natural man understandeth not the things of God." These are only spiritually discerned.

At midnight the scene on Gerizim becomes once more all animation. Little children, fully dressed, are shaken out of their sleep by their elders. They yawn, stretch themselves, and stand up in readiness for the feast. The priests now unseal the oven, and the carcasses are taken out all crisp and sizzling. The smell of roast meat pervades the chilly air, making the mouth water. There is no morsel for us; only we have food for thought.

The glowing oven, just opened, instead of consuming, has now returned its contents in the form of nourishment and savory refreshment. Here we have still another type of the One who emerged from the fierce oven of Golgotha, unconsumed and in resurrection power, as the Heavenly Manna, the Bread of Life, the Paschal Lamb upon whom we feed by simple faith and communion.

It was indeed an interesting sight to watch these Samaritans, especially the little children with muffled faces, standing to eat the meat of the Passover. Even the tiny tots knew how to tear the smoking flesh apart with their little fingers, while we looked on, almost with envy. There was ample meat for all except the stranger. At the end of the meal, the bones were all carefully collected and burned. All seemed happy and satisfied at the consummation of another feast on Gerizim, and soon began to settle down comfortably for the remainder of the night. When, at last, the day dawned upon the scene, not one vestige of the sacrifice remained…

There are two very ancient parchment rolls of the Pentateuch in the possession of the Samaritans at Nablous. One of these is claimed to be the oldest scroll of the Law in existence. They are very proud of this possession, and will show it to visitors who go to see their little synagogue. Being poor, they will gladly accept even the smallest gift. Like the Jews, they are suffering today for the sin of their forefathers in rejecting the light of the gospel. The spiritual revival, which began with the saving of the woman at Jacob's Well, and which seemed well on the way to spreading to the Samaritan community, might well have changed the history of these people. Just how this revival was checked, and by whom, will never be known till a coming day. Yet somehow, the Gospel light kindled by the Lord Himself at Sychar's Well was quenched; and so the Samaritans still stubbornly continue with the Passover on Gerizim.

Not all the blood of beasts on Jewish altars slain
Could give the guilty conscience peace or wash away one stain.

But Christ, the heavenly Lamb, took all our sins away,
A sacrifice of nobler name and richer blood than they.

Our souls look back to see the burden Thou didst bear
When made a curse upon the tree, for all our guilt was there.

Believing, we rejoice to see the curse remove;
We bless the Lamb with cheerful voice, and sing redeeming love.   —Isaac Watts

—J. W. Clapham in *Palestine: Land of My Adoption*, dated 1946, pp. 90-95. Mr. James Clapham was a New Zealand school teacher who stopped in Palestine in 1926 en route to the U. K. Deeply burdened by the lack of gospel light in the Middle East, he remained. Pitching a tent wherever he went, he was used by the Lord to see New Testament assemblies established in Haifa, Jerusalem, Jaffa, and Tel Aviv, Israel; Nicosia, Cyprus; Beirut, Lebanon; Damascus, Aleppo, and Antioch, Syria; Istanbul, Turkey (he visited Smyrna, Ephesus, Sardis, and Laodicea, but found no response to the gospel); and worked intermittently in Egypt from 1936 to 1951.

H. A. Ironside at Jacob's Well

At Nablus,…the Shechem of the Bible, we spent about half-an-hour, threading our way through its dirty, narrow, winding streets to find the Samaritan synagogue. We entered it and found a very kind old Samaritan gentleman, the last high priest of that tribe, who succeeded to the priesthood about a year-and-a-half ago when his predecessor died. He told us a little about the history of his people, and how they still observe the Passover. He showed us a very ancient scroll written on parchment, which he declared was written by the grandson of Moses. We had our doubts about that, but did not think it polite to express them. It was at least very interesting. I examined the Hebrew letters, and they were not the square ones which have been in use for many centuries but were of a much more ancient type.

After leaving the Samaritan priest, as we went out of the city, our attention was drawn to Mount Gerizim and Mount Ebal—Mount Gerizim, where certain of the Levites stood to bless the people, and Mount Ebal where others stood to pronounce the curse if they departed from the living God. We felt we must be very near the well where Jesus met the woman of Samaria. Soon we drew near a little city and I asked its name. It was Sychar. John tells us: "And He must needs go through Samaria, Then cometh He to a city of Samaria, called. Sychar, near to the parcel of ground that Jacob gave to his son Joseph." Joseph himself was buried there. We did not have far to look to see his sepulcher, and our guide said, "There is Joseph's tomb. We Mohammedans think just as much of that as the Jews and Christians do, and it has been undisturbed through the centuries." It was interesting indeed to know that in all likelihood the body of Joseph was actually still preserved within that tomb.

A local woman at Jacob's well

Abraham, Sarah, Isaac, Rebekah, Jacob, and Leah are buried in Machpelah, at Hebron, but Joseph was buried in the plot of ground given him by his father. Soon the voice of the Lord will be heard and they shall all rise to meet Him, with all the redeemed, in the air. What a moment that will be!

We passed on from Joseph's tomb and just ahead saw an inclosed garden and a little Greek chapel within. Our guide told us that Jacob's well was inside the chapel. It always provoked us to find these chapels over so many of the places of special interest. Almost every site of this kind is covered over either with a Roman Catholic church or a Greek or Armenian chapel. However, we entered the chapel and saw the well itself. It is built up about two feet from the ground with the coping, as when Jesus sat there so long ago. I am not sure, of course, that it is not actually the same coping as the one on which He sat, but it seems very old and they have built another wall of stone around it to keep it from falling to pieces. We sat there and looked into its depths. We could not see very far down in the darkness, but a Syrian woman brought a candle with a long cord on it, and after we had given her a few piasters she dropped it down nearly a hundred feet, and there we could see the water in the bottom of the well. We understood what the woman of Samaria meant when she said, "Thou hast nothing to draw with, and the well is deep: from whence then hast Thou that living water?"

—H. A. Ironside in *Things Seen and Heard in Bible Lands* of a trip to Palestine in 1936, pp. 67-70

A. E. Booth at Bethel

We are now having it very rough and rocky, over hills, through ravines and narrow passes, with abundance of stones forming obstacles in our way, but we are nearing Bethel, and as we journey on we pass immense and beautifully terraced olive-yards. Ephraim all through these parts answers well to its name "fruitful" and if properly cultivated would yield very much more.

We much admire the beautiful way in which the sides of these hills are terraced, to preserve the rich soil from being washed away.

We have at last reached Bethel, Jacob's ancient resting-place (Gen. 28), and this evening, if we were minded, like Jacob, to lay down our weary heads to rest, we should not require to go far to get a pillow similar to his, for they are everywhere around us. Stones! stones! scarce anything but stones! Here and there a patch of grass, where a few sheep and goats feed beside their attendant shepherd-boy; but the predominating feature of the scenery in this part is—stones.

Here George points out the place where the bears came and devoured the children in the days of Elisha (2 Ki. 2:23-24).

Bethel was the place where Jacob received his wonderful vision, and God's pledge to bless and keep His servant just on the eve of his departure from this land; this was grace, all grace; but it was also the place where God executed judgment upon those who abused His faithful prophet. In either case we might add Jacob's words: "How dreadful is this place, it is none other but the house of God, and this is the gate of heaven."

At this place our hearts beat fast, for there in the distance we see a hill surmounted by a tower which glitters in the rays of the setting sun. It is the Mount of

The Booth party heading south on the road between Shechem & Bethel

Olives, which we gaze on for the first time. Towards the east we see the Dead Sea, and beyond we can clearly discern the mountains of Moab.

We have strange feelings tonight for only another night, and if all goes well we shall be in Jerusalem. We are all very tired, and our ponies proceed to Ramallah, where it is supposed the company halted as they journeyed from Jerusalem to Nazareth, in Luke 2:41-51; there they found that Jesus was not in their midst. Here we entered a hotel and were well accommodated for the night; and after our evening meal we walked out to visit a Christian mission, where we conversed on the Lord's work in these parts. One of our party read Luke 2, and added a few words, after which some of us engaged in prayer and praise, and returned to the hotel thankful to have been where a few of the Lord's dear people labor, seeking to teach and preach Jesus Christ.

—A. E. Booth in *The Land Far Off*, recording a trip to Palestine and Egypt in April of 1905, pp. 98-100

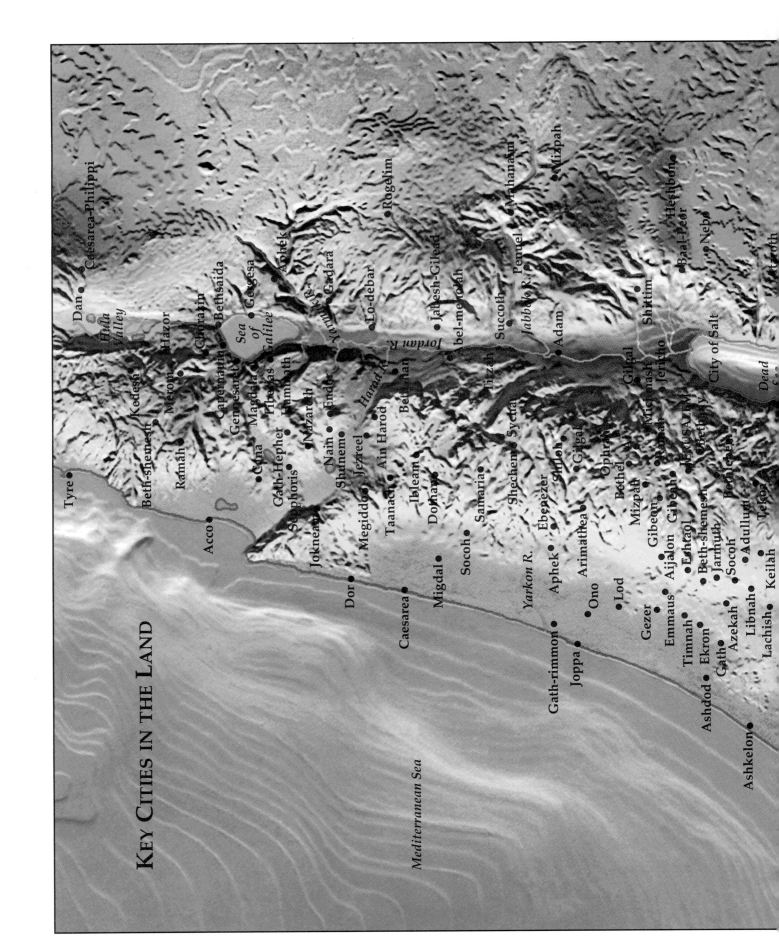

KEY CITIES IN THE LAND

Mediterranean Sea

Tyre

Caesarea-Philippi

Dan
Hula Valley
Hazor
Kedesh
Beth-shemesh
Meron
Ramah
Chorazin
Capernaum
Bethsaida
Gennesaret
Magdala
Gergesa
Tiberias
Sea of Galilee
Aphek
Hammath
Cana
Gath-Hepher
Nazareth
Endor
Gadara
Sepphoris
Nain
Shunem
Jezreel
Ain Harod
Harod R.
Bethshan
Lo-debar
Jabesh-Gilead
Abel-meholah
Tirzah
Succoth
Jabbok R.
Adam
Acco
Jokneam
Megiddo
Taanach
Ibleam
Dotham
Samaria
Shechem
Sychar
Ophrah
Rogelim
Mahanaim
Penuel
Mizpah
Shittim
Heshbon
Nebo
Baal-peor
Dor
Migdal
Socoh
Ebenezer
Shiloh
Gilgal
Bethel
Mizpah
Michmash
Jericho
Beth
Gilgal
City of Salt
Caesarea
Aphek
Arimathea
Ono
Lod
Gibeon
Gibeah
JERUSALEM
Dead Sea
Gath-rimmon
Joppa
Yarkon R.
Emmaus
Aijalon
Eshtaol
Beth-shemesh
Jarmuth
Bethlehem
Tekoa
Gezer
Timnah
Ekron
Socoh
Adullam
Ashdod
Gath
Azekah
Libnah
Keilah
Lachish
Ashkelon
Jordan R.
Yarmuk R.

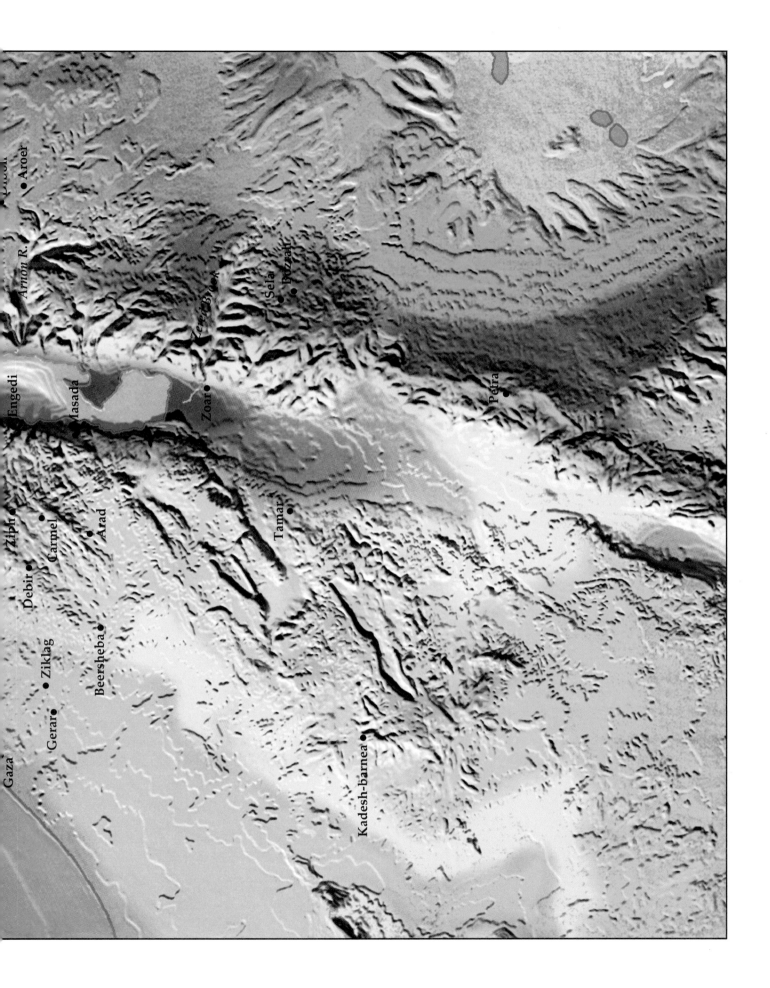

The North & Central Coastal Plains

*L*eaving behind the naturally fortified Samaritan highlands, we descend westward into the coastal plain. If you recall, the coastal plain forms one of four narrow north-south landforms in Israel: the Coastal Plain, the Central Highlands, the Jordan Rift Valley, and the Eastern Plateau across the Jordan.

The plain stretches along the sea for almost 200 miles from Wadi el-Arish on the edge of the desert to Rosh HaNiqra (the Ladder of Tyre in ancient times) on the traditional border between Lebanon and Israel. The plain in the south is 20 miles wide and continues to narrow until it is pinched off by a promontory of the Galilee range that reaches the sea.

Three natural boundaries divide the coast into four regions. The Asher plain extends from Rosh HaNiqra to Mount Carmel; the Dor plain from Mount Carmel to the Crocodile Swamps just north of New Testament Caesarea; the Sharon plain continues south to the Yarkon River; and the plains of Philistia complete the coastal landscape as they meld into the desert (the Wilderness of Shur).

The Plain of Asher in the north, apart from the city of Acco or Ptolemais, has little biblical significance. At Acco there was an assembly visited by Paul once. Asher was unable to conquer and hold this region in the days of the Judges.

The same could be said for the relative unimportance of the Plain of Dor. Contained on the north by the Carmel Range and on the south by the swamps, it was apparently covered with scrub thickets. Only the city of Dor had any significance in the Scriptures. An ancient royal Canaanite city, its king was slain by Joshua's forces (Josh. 11:2; 12:23; 17:11), but later the tribe of Manasseh could not drive out its inhabitants (Jud. 1:27). It is to be remembered that Israel was forbidden the use of chariots which were ideally suited for maneuvering in the flat, open areas. In the mountains, such conveyances were virtually useless. Therefore Israel took and held the high country and left the lowlands for the Canaanites who were left to plague them all their days.

What irony, then, that the territory given to the state of Israel by the UN-approved partitioning of the land—the coast and interior lowlands—was the very area they had been unable to conquer at first.

Later, the area of Dor was tributary to both David and Solomon (1 Ki. 4:11; 1 Chron. 7:29). One of Solomon's regional officers, the son of Abinidab, was stationed in this area and was responsible for the royal victuals for one month out of the year. We are told as well that this man was also Solomon's son-in-law. The region further south, including the two population centers in the Shechem valley—Hepher and Socoh—was also a Solomonic region.

This seems ordinary enough, that coastal lands with good rainfall should be fertile farmland. Was this not the sub-tropical paradise from which the rose of Sharon derived its name? But the Plains of Sharon are not naturally fertile. They are composed of Mousterian sand which tends to hold water just underground. This accentuates the high water table, producing a quagmire. Until World War I, the area was covered with small scrub, used by the Turks to fuel their railway.

When the Jewish National Fund started reclaiming the land, this was malaria-infested swamp. But it was soon discovered by the indefatigable Israelis that, once drained, it provided the ideal ingredients for citrus growing. Its famed Jaffa oranges now grow here in profusion along with other citrus crops, avocados, and bananas in abundance.

So it is that Sharon plain, when left to itself, degenerates into a slough of despond. Isaiah speaks of a day then future when Sharon would be "like a wilderness" (Isa. 33:9). The rose of Sharon would be beauty surrounded by ugliness. Only during the days of Solomon do we read of this land being fruitful. And so it was that when the "greater than Solomon" came, it was to a people devastated by sin, a moral wilderness. There He stooped and began the tender cultivation of His Bride, the rose of Sharon. Still planted here in the world's waste, we who know Him have the honor of letting "the beauty of the Lord God be upon us" (Ps. 90:17). It is a sad and ruined world. When someone stops "to smell the roses," it may be the fragrance of your life that turns their thoughts to God.

Joppa and the Beautiful Gospel

The foam-crested waves of the azure Mediterranean have cast themselves on the shores of Israel through the centuries. The tides of war, too, have washed across this land, shaping its history as the oceans have shaped its shoreline. To the north, the land of Phoenicia has deep, natural harbors at Beirut, Tripolis, Ugarit, and Zarephath. But the Israeli coast, called a concordant shore, runs almost parallel to the principle mountain range that forms the backbone of the land. The extremely regular shore provides no natural harbors along its length.

Thus the Phoenicians became the travellers, and the Israelites became the traders, exchanging their agricultural products at the coastal town of Joppa. South of Joppa, the Philistines utilized the cove at Ashkelon and there was another barely useable cove at Dor.

Later, just before New Testament times, Herod the Great enlarged the anchorage at Strato's Tower by building an artificial harbor that included an expansive breakwater. Its construction was an engineering marvel, incorporating the first extensive use of hydraulic concrete and an anti-siltation system.

But Joppa was the major seaport in ancient Israel. Jaffa, or Yafo, as it is called today, means "beautiful." And, says the Scriptures, *"How beautiful upon the mountains are the feet of him that bringeth good tidings, that publisheth peace; that bringeth good tidings of good, that publisheth salvation"* (Isa. 52:7). It was God's purpose that His people Israel would take the news of the one true God to all the world, *"and in thee shall all families of the earth be blessed"* (Gen. 12:3).

The Israelites, however, were not travellers (until forced to be in the great *diasporas*). Therefore the tribe that was given Joppa would be those privileged with spreading the news of the one true God to the ends of the earth. Who were they?

"And the seventh lot came out for the tribe of Dan…And the coast of their inheritance was [among other places]*…Japho* (Joppa). *And the coast of the children of Dan went out too little for them: therefore the children of Dan went up to fight against Leshem, and took it…and called Leshem, Dan, after the name of Dan their father"* (Josh. 19:40-47). Unwilling or unable to live in the land allotted to them, many of the Danites settled in the extreme north of Israel, under the shadow of Mount Hermon. There, instead of telling of the one true God to the nations, they were the first tribe to institutionalize idolatry, adopting the gods of the nations for themselves. Dan eventually became Pan, the shrine-laden rock face dedicated to myriad gods.

But God does not give up. If the Jews would not take the message of good news to the Gentiles, He would build a house of prayer for all nations and the Gentiles would come seeking Him. So it was that cedars from Lebanon were floated along the coast from Byblos to Joppa for Solomon's temple. With a hint of the true temple to come (Eph. 2:11-22), the structure was composed of Jewish stones and Gentile timbers, and the man who oversaw the construction was half Jew (his mother was from Dan), and half Gentile (2 Chron. 2:14). And Gentiles *did* come seeking the true God: the Queen of Sheba, the Ethiopian eunuch, Cornelius, Simon the Cyrene, and others.

Nonetheless, Joppa continued to stand as the gateway of the gospel. The Mediterranean (the troubled sea which pictured the nations never at rest) drew ships from around the ancient world to the harbor there. And Jonah, commissioned by God to take His message to Nineveh, fled there to catch a ship to anywhere—anywhere but Nineveh.

Hundreds of years later, the son of another Jonah sat overlooking the same harbor when he saw a tarpaulin, full of unclean animals, and heard the command: "Rise, Peter, kill and eat." There the Lord prepared Peter to take the second key (he had used the first at Pentecost) to open the door to the Gentiles at the house of Cornelius in Caesarea (Acts 9:43-10:16).

One of the most effective witnesses at Joppa was Dorcas, or Tabitha (Acts 9:36-42). Through her life, death, and resuscitation, "many believed in the Lord" (v. 42). Are both her Jewish and Gentile names given because she at last was fulfilling the desire of our large-hearted God who is *"not willing that any should perish, but that all should come to repentance"* (2 Pet. 3:9)? Are we?

The Land of Philistia

As noted in a previous chapter, the 190-mile coastal plain that runs the length of the western border of Israel is divided into smaller regions by natural boundaries. The most southerly region, the Plains of Philistia, were bounded on the north by the Yarkon River at Joppa and on the south by Wadi el-Arish, approximately 50 miles south of Gaza.

The plain is relatively flat. That, in Bible times, was both a bane and a blessing. It was, on the one hand, fertile, easily tilled farmland, composed of heavy alluvial soil carried down from the Shephela (foothills). Abundant fresh water springs rise out of the hills and add their enriching influence to the plain. But there was a disadvantage to such open land. Unless fortified by walled cities and protected by lightning-fast charioteers (forbidden to Israel), it was in constant danger of being overrun. Compounding the problem, it is to be remembered that the ideal land route linking Africa with Europe or Asia was right through this territory. It was constantly being trampled underfoot by marauding armies.

Who were the Philistines? Whoever they were, and debate swirls around the issue, they were not philistines. The word philistine, especially when not capitalized, is used derogatorily to describe an uninformed individual who has no time for intellectual or artistic pursuits. Archaeologists continue to be amazed as they uncover the five chief cities of the Philistines: Ashkelon, Ashdod, Gaza, Gath, and Ekron.

Ashkelon is the site of one of the oldest cities in the world. Within the mound can be found the remnants of six civilizations, one built on top of the other—Canaanite, Philistine, Greco-Roman, Byzantine, Moslem, and Crusader. It is now suggested that the Philistines or "Sea Peoples" arrived here in the 12th Century BC, after attempting to overcome the Egyptian domination of the region. However the Scriptures record a Philistine presence here much earlier. In Deuteronomy 2:23, the original inhabitants of this region are referred to as Avvim, but were dispossessed by "the Caphtorim, that came forth out of Caphtor." Jeremiah adds that the Philistines were "the remnant of the isle of Caphtor" (47:4). Caphtor is generally taken to be Crete or the seacoast area of Asia Minor. However, it is also suggested that their origins were from Egypt (see Gen. 10:13-14; Mizraim is the ancient name for Egypt).

Abraham and Isaac are said to have dealt with the Philistines (Gen. 21:32; 26:16). The early relationship between the Hebrews and the Philistines seems relatively friendly, in fact until the conquest in the days of Joshua. By this time they had grown strong, having formed their fabled five-city alliance and were part of the "very much land to be possessed"—the unfinished business of the conquest at the time of Joshua's death (Josh. 13:1-3). Judah then ventured a raid against them, but it was repulsed (Jud. 1:18-19), and the Philistine attacks on Israel's southern flank became increasingly devastating until they dominated the land for 40 years (Jud. 13:1).

The days of Samson and his lusty deeds (was he coming this time to kill their men or ravish their women?) paint a vivid portrait of Philistia: wheat fields, olive groves, and vineyards (for which Ashkelon was famous), lavish temples and fortified cities with bronze gates, not to mention their seductive women and pagan rites that captured more than a few of Israel's hearts.

Even Samson's own tribe did not follow him and Israel's relief from the oppression of the Philistines was temporary at best. The blind deliverer (whose name means *sunshine*) ended his life in the dark, as Milton wrote concerning him:

> *O dark, dark, dark, amid the blaze of noon,*
> *Irrecoverably dark, total eclipse without all hope of day.*

Well, not quite! "O Lord God," he prayed, "strengthen me, I pray Thee, only this once, O God..." (Jud. 16:28). The God of one more chance heard the cry and "the dead which he slew at his death were more than they which he slew in his life" (v. 30). Yet the early chapters of 1 Samuel are filled with twenty more years of Philistine domination. It was not until God found a true champion in David that the soldiers from Philistia learned to flee before Israel and her God.

The history of the coastal Philistine plain is written all in bold face. Here is the land of conflict with men who are not afraid to "throw their weight around." Here Isaac was turned away from water rights that had been established in the days of his father (it was good for the Philistines that it was not his contentious son, Jacob!). Leaving to the infidels their Esek and Sitnah (meaning "contention" and "enmity"), Isaac found his Rehoboth where, said he, "Now the Lord hath made room for us" (Gen. 26:19-22). We would do well to follow Isaac and let the world fight its own battles. Let the Lord fight for us. He knows how to make room for His people.

Here also Joshua engaged the Canaanite enemy in the first battle for Israel in wide-open terrain—the finger valleys that ran down toward the sea. He had been called to protect the Gibeonites whose city sat on a ridge between the Aijalon Valley and the Beth-horon Pass. Willing to keep his word, even to his own hurt, Joshua force-marched his men at night through the wilderness of Judea, rising from 1200 feet below sea level to more than 2500 feet above. He arrived at dawn just in time to engage the enemy.

The Southern Confederacy was forced to flee before the God of Israel, who utilized the forces of nature (which the Philistines worshipped). The sun and moon conspired with a man that day. Hailstones also aided Israel in the battle. The southern kings sought refuge in a cave near the town of Makkedah (thought by some to be present-day el-Mughar). The cave became their jail when Israel found them and covered the mouth with a great stone. When the people had assembled, the cave was opened and the kings made to lie in the dust. Then Joshua called for representatives of the troops to place their heels on the necks of the condemned rulers, sharing the joy of victory with his faithful men.

The battle lines ebbed and flowed between Philistia and Judea in the subsequent years. As noted, Samson won—and lost—against the big men. Unfortunately, he was only big on the outside. His use of raw strength is not the way to do exploits for God. By contrast, David championed the cause of the Lord by taking up the challenge hurled against the quivering populace of Israel. It must have caused at least a momentary shudder in Goliath's heart when the strippling, approaching with his sling at the ready, calmly informed his enemy, "Today I'm coming to avenge your defiance of God. I will be removing your head in the process." So he did, in the name of God.

As the sad years passed, Saul retreated into himself while David continued to prove God, storming the strongholds of the enemy, and taking territory for the expansion of the kingdom. I understand there are numerous openings for the same work today (2 Cor. 10:3-4).

The Elah Valley, battlefield between David and Goliath, with the Philistines near Azekah (left), Israel to the right.

The Final Victory

We have considered the geography of the coastal region of Philistia in southwest Israel (now known politically as the Gaza Strip) and some of its history up to the end of the Judges. Most of these skirmishes ended in defeat for the Israelites. And little changed with the demise of the judges.

You will recall the suicidal foray by the Israeli militia with the two corrupt sons of Eli, Hophni and Phinehas, bringing the ark of the covenant to the battlefield as a kind of good-luck charm. The intent was to motivate the Jews to fight, but the resulting war cry was so blood-curdling to the Philistines' ears that the whole experiment turned counter-productive. It was the Philistines who took the God of Israel seriously, defeating their foe (including the destruction of the house of Eli), and capturing the ark. This they removed to the temple of their fish-man god, Dagon. Not knowing the command, "Thou shalt have no other gods before Me," they left the idol and the ark in the darkness of their shrine overnight.

In the morning, Dagon lay on his face. So what do you do when your god falls over? Prop him back up, I suppose! And that is just what they did. But the next morning, Dagon lay shattered. Broken off were its head and hands (that in which man glories—what he thinks and what he does), and all that was left was the "fishy" part. The Philistines seemed to get the point. They had come face to face with the true God. It reminded them of the story they had heard about the destruction of Egypt when Pharoah had defied Jehovah. But instead of running to Him, they ran away from Him, sending the ark back on a new cart, pulled by two milk cows, to Israel. Can you then understand why God became upset when Uzzah touched the ark? He was just trying to help! But the Lord God, the Creator of heaven and earth, doesn't need to be propped up. He is the one who holds us up, not the other way around.

But we're getting ahead of our story. David had dealings with the Philistines long before he brought the ark up to Jerusalem (or at least to nearby Gibeon). As a young man, he had been sent to bring his brothers victuals while they were serving in Saul's army. The journey was not a long one from Bethlehem to the Valley of Elah. The Elah runs roughly east-west, forming a natural corridor from the coastal plain to the cities sitting along the mountainous spine through the center of the land.

When David arrived at the battle site, he discovered that Goliath of Gath had challenged Israel to produce a champion to engage in one-on-one mortal combat. The winner would provide his army with a sure victory over the other side. Now Israel had pled for a king for this very reason. It was not enough that Jehovah had led them into battle; they wanted a big man that they could see! Well, where is he now? He has come up against a *colossal* man and Saul is hiding in his tent. God must bring his man from the sheep cotes to deliver Israel.

It is often assumed that David refused Saul's armor because it was ungainly, several sizes too large. But the Scripture does not say that. It states David's objection as being: "I cannot go with these; I have not *proved* them." What had he proved? "I come to you in the name of the Lord God of Israel…" he declared. It was God who had delivered him from the lion and the bear, and God alone he would trust now.

Jonathan—swifter than an eagle, stronger than a lion, as David described him—had won his own victories against this perennial foe (1 Sam. 14). Leading his armorbearer up the craggy height to the enemy, Jonathan proved the principle certainly needed in our day: "There is no restraint to the Lord to save by many or by few" (v. 6). God give us more Jonathans today.

While Saul either lounged under a pomegranate tree at Gibeah, or hunted David like game, David drove back the Philistine army time and again (1 Sam. 18:27; 19:8; 23:5). Of course he was not there when the Philistines slaughtered Israel on the slopes of Gilboa, including the house of Saul.

Later as king, David pushed back this human tidal wave once and again (2 Sam. 5:20; 5:22; etc.). Yet the Israelites never completely subjugated these big men, these uncircumcised Gentiles. Does that sound familiar? (See Eph. 4:17.) But victory was finally assured to Israel: "I will cut off the pride of the Philistine" (Zech. 9:6) . So is victory assured to us; the day is coming when, free of the flesh, we will serve the Lord as we ought.

The Shephela

Even a hurried look at the map of Israel shows that the country flares out as it moves to the south. The eastern border, following the Jordan Rift Valley, runs almost due south, and the central mountain ridge roughly follows the river. But the Mediterranean coastline sweeps in a J toward the Nile delta. The coastal plain does widen some as it moves toward the Negev (the southern deserts), but this still leaves a wedge of land between the Gaza Strip (plains of Philistia) and the Judean Highlands, 5-8 miles wide. This region is known as the *shephela*. It is, says Howard Kitchen, that "sloping moorland with ridges of rocks and a loose gathering of chalk and limestone hills, round, bare, and featureless."

The shephela, or foothills are divided from the mountains of Judea by a trough composed of two wadis or seasonal riverbeds (Wadi Sar and Wadi Ghurab). Beginning at the Aijalon Valley, this region of soft limestone hills runs 30 miles south almost to the Brook Besor, east of Gaza.

The Hebrew word, *shephela,* is translated in the Authorized Version* by the words low country, plain, or valley and comes from a root meaning "to humiliate." As will be noted, its history lives up (or perhaps down) to its etymology as a region where those who defied the God of heaven were soundly humiliated.

The undulating hills are interspersed with a series of finger valleys that, since ancient times to the present, have provided natural thoroughfares from the coast up to the mountain fortresses in the high country. These also became impromptu battlefields since the shephela was the buffer between the five cities of the Philistines and the Israelites in Judah. It also contained Amorite strongholds like Lachish, Libnah, and Jarmuth. Whoever dominated at the time controlled this territory.

It was in the Aijalon Valley that the southern Amorite confederacy under Adoni-zedec, king of Jerusalem, arrayed themselves against the fledgling alliance between Joshua and the crafty Gibeonites. With a plea for help coming late in the day from those who had recently deceived him, Joshua might well have delayed until morning. But, says the record, "Joshua ascended (3500 feet in 20 miles!) from Gilgal...all night" (Josh. 10:7, 9). He arrived with his troops just in time to engage the enemy at dawn, coming "unto them suddenly." Then, after being up the day before, an all-night march, and hand-to-hand combat all the next day, he called on the sun to stay its course so he could finish the job!

Then it was that the enemy fled before them, making the Israelites chase their enemy up hill and down dale, as far as Azekah in the Elah Valley. Only then did the people taste the sweetness of total victory, placing their heels on the necks of the enemy generals. How prescient of the coming day when the One who crushed the Serpent's head (Gen. 3:15) will "bruise Satan under your heel" (Rom. 16:20).

Samson, laid low in the Sorek, next valley to the south, discovered that the Lord does not have two sets of rules, one for His enemies and one for His fair-haired sons. Thankfully, the Lord gave him another chance: in death, he laid low 3,000 Philistines and their idol, Dagon.

The Elah Valley, further south yet, ran up to Bethlehem, David's hometown. The day it echoed with the defiant curses of Goliath, young David responded: "This day will the Lord deliver thee into mine hand; and I will smite thee, and take thine head from thee...that all the earth may know that there is a God in Israel." Moments later, the Gentile champion lay, face down, on the ground. Later, David would find refuge at nearby Adullam from the raging Saul, who allowed the root of bitterness to find fertile ground in his heart the day they sang: "Saul has slain his thousands, but..." The root would grow into a mighty tree full of rancid fruit that would overshadow his life, blocking out the sun and withering his soured soul until what was left of his life collapsed, uprooted, twice dead, on the slopes of Gilboa, a warning to us all (Heb. 12:15).

---

* Here is a complete listing of occurrences of the word *shephela* in the KJV. *valleys:* Josh. 9:1; 10:40; 11:2, 16; 12:8; 15:33; Jud. 1:9; *low plains, low country:* 1 Chron. 27:28; 2 Chron. 9:27; 26:10; 28:18; *the valley, the vale:* Deut. 1:7; 1 Ki. 10:27; 2 Chron. 1:15; Jer. 32:44; 33:13; *the plain:* Jer. 17:26; Zech. 7:7; and Obad. 1:19.

Photo: *A herd of dromedaries not far from Beersheba. Looking south toward the Negev.*
Inset: *Still in many villages in the spring can be seen the separating of the wheat from the chaff by winnowing.*

The Negev

The name of the desert land on the southern extremity of the occupied regions of Israel has shifted as surely as the sands swept by the winds across its moon-like surface. The Hebrew spelling is Negeb, but the popular usage, Negev, follows the pronunciation of the word instead. Mentioned over one hundred times in the Old Testament, it is rendered "south" even though its meaning is "dryness."

This provides the key to such strange passages as Genesis 13:1 where we read that "Abram went up out of Egypt into the south." Of course we know he was travelling northeast, but his journey took him into the area south of the habitable parts of Judah.

The Negev falls roughly into three areas. The southern Negev conforms approximately to the biblical wilderness of Paran (Num. 10:12; Deut. 1:1; 1 Sam. 25:1). Virtually uninhabited even by the hardy Bedouins, it is almost lifeless, resourceless, and without vegetation till the present. Here Ishmael, the wild son of the bondwoman, dwelt (Gen. 21:21).

The central Negev was known in the Old Testament as the wilderness of Zin (see Num. 20:1; 34:3; Josh. 15:1). It too is so barren today that even flocks used to paltry grazing cannot find enough to survive. But to the careful observer there is evidence that some diligent optimists thought there was hope in this "great and terrible wilderness" (Deut. 8:15). In *Holy Fields*, Howard Kitchen writes the following:

"Energetic schemes of irrigation and water conservancy were carried out in this district by Christian settlers from AD 400 onwards until they were driven out by the Mohammedan invasions of the seventh century. The remains of some of their dams and reservoirs have recently been found, and in the ruins of their church buildings have been recovered many ancient papyrus documents preserved by the dryness of the climate. On similar irrigation schemes are founded the hope of present-day Jews planning to revive the dreary wastes of the Negev…. Jewish settlements in the [northern] Negev have shown remarkable progress; orchards, vineyards, vegetable gardens, and wheat fields now occupy thousands of acres of what was once desert."

The northern Negev receives some uncertain rainfall, perhaps ten inches annually. The basins where Beersheba and Arad gather the run-off have been long settled. These two centers have a colorful history. Beersheba (*well of the oath,* see Gen. 21:25-33; 22:19; 26:23-25; 46:1-5) was the dwelling of Abraham in his old age where the oath—which gave the place its name—was made between Abraham and Abimelech. From here the patriarch left with Isaac for the memorial journey to Moriah. Today you can peer into the depths of the ancient well at Beersheba which dates back to patriarchal times.

Later, Isaac lived in the Negev, at Beersheba, Beer-lahairoi, and Gerar. It was also from here that Jacob fled his brother and to which he returned, not after "a few days" (Gen. 27:44) but many years. He never again was able to see the mother to whom he was the favorite. Also, as an old man, he stopped here en route to Egypt at Joseph's invitation, where he was reassured by God to continue the journey.

Arad (or Zephath) lies 10 miles east-northeast of Beersheba at the south end of the Judean mountains. This city's army drove the Israelites away when they attempted an ill-fated attack, after being turned back into the desert for their unbelief (Num. 14:45). Then, near the end of their wanderings, they pitched again at Kadesh; again Arad attacked, taking prisoners. It led to Arad's utter destruction; then God renamed it Hormah, from a root meaning *accursed* or *devoted to destruction* (Num. 21:1-3). Today the ruins of Tell Arad remind us that God takes it seriously when someone touches the apple of His eye.

When the land was finally subdued, Moses' Kenite relatives settled in the central Negev and Caleb's daughter, Achsah, and son-in-law/brother, Othniel, received a section there as a wedding present. Subsequently, Achsah also requested—and received—springs to turn her desert into a garden (Jud. 1:13-17). She was a true chip off the old block; like Caleb, Achsah wanted all that God would give her.

God give us more Othniels and Achsahs: longing for all God has for them; driving out the enemy; turning wastelands into gardens by welcoming the life-giving influence of the upper and the nether springs (Jn. 4:14; 7:37-39).

Down to the Dead Sea

rom the Judean ridge we begin our descent toward the eerie moonscapes at the Dead Sea. Going east over Olivet, we pass Bethany, home of Mary, Martha, and Lazarus—one of the few places where the Lord received true fellowship, service, and worship. No wonder He chose to go Home from there (Lk. 24:50-55). Suddenly we come face to face with the stark reality of the Judean wilderness. Working carefully along the dizzying edge of Wadi Kelt, we follow a serpentine road barely as wide as our vehicle, dropping 1700 feet in 22 miles! When the Lord said, "A man went *down* from Jerusalem," it was no exaggeration. With relief we make one last turn and, surprisingly, a carpet of green stretches before us.

It is Jericho, city of palms, largest oasis and lowest city in the world. With ruins that date back almost 10,000 years, it is one of the oldest cities as well. The ancient site, located at Tell es-Sultan, was blessed with a copious spring and strategically located at the gateway to the heartland of Canaan.

Home of Rahab, it came under Joshua's curse, a curse reaped 500 years later by the foolish Hiel of Bethel in the days of godless Ahab (Josh. 6:26; 1 Ki. 16:34). Jericho was also the site of Ehud's victory over Eglon of Moab (Jud. 3:13-15), and the place where Elisha cured the brackish waters (2 Ki. 2:18-22). New Testament Jericho (a slightly different location) also figures in the Saviour's ministry: here he healed two blind men, one of whom was Bartimaeus (Mk. 10:46), and here the Master visited the home of Zacchaeus, a cursed man from a cursed city in a cursed profession who received the blessing of God.

John Garstang led a dig here from 1930 to 1936. He concluded that the evidence of a conflagration and his dating of the city's end at c. 1400 BC, fit exactly with the biblical account in Joshua 6. He wrote: "In all material details and in date the fall of Jericho took place as described in the Biblical narrative." But archeologist Dame Kathleen Kenyon, who followed him (1952-1958), denied that such a walled city was here when Joshua led Israel into the land. Her conclusions (published without her data) were heralded as key evidence to show that the biblical record of historical events was flawed at best. The fact was, however, that Kenyon's *evidence* was not published until some years after her death. This data, recently released, does not agree with her conclusions. In fact, as scholar Bryant Wood has shown, her work has uncovered the biblical story exactly. She describes the wall as having collapsed outward, providing a ramp up into the city. Her photographs show the large supplies of grain found, corroborating the Bible account that the city did not fall after a long siege, was captured at harvest time, and that Jericho was a burnt offering to the Lord. Wood applauds Kenyon's "careful and painstaking field work." But he shows her accumulated evidence, rather than disproving the biblical record, actually verifies it.

Keep blowing the trumpet! The blessed old Book is as dependable now as the day it came to us from the heart of God. Which brings us to our next stop. Just eight miles south of Jericho lie the ruins of Qumran, cloaked in mystery. Theories abound as to who lived here. But our interest is concerned with some caves across the gorge where, in 1947, the fabled Dead Sea scrolls were discovered. More than 2,000 years old, they show that the God who supernaturally gave His Word also supernaturally preserved it. When brain surgeons helped to carefully unroll these ancient copies of the Hebrew Scriptures, and scholars laid them up against the Bible as we had it, there was not one significant change!

On our way south along the western shore of the Dead Sea, we will pass Engedi ("spring of the wild goats"), where David hid from envy-mad Saul (1 Sam. 23:29), and where later his son, Solomon, would plant tropical gardens (Song of Sol. 1:14). Some day, when the river of God, flowing from Messiah's throne in Jerusalem, cures the Dead Sea, they will set their nets here (Ezek. 47:10).

A stop at the tepid saline sea (27% salts) does little to refresh our bodies but much to refresh our minds. Called in the Bible the Salt, or Eastern Sea, the Dead Sea is 11 by 47 miles. This is the lowest spot on the surface of the earth—1292 feet below sea level. Is there something symbolic in this? It certainly was the scene of one of the low marks in history. We remember Lot's wife, remember that God turned "Sodom and Gomorrha into ashes…making them an example to all those that after should live ungodly." But we remember, too, that the Lord knows how to deliver the godly out of temptations (2 Pet. 2:6-9).

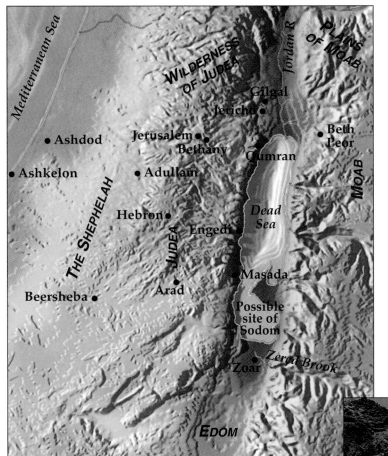

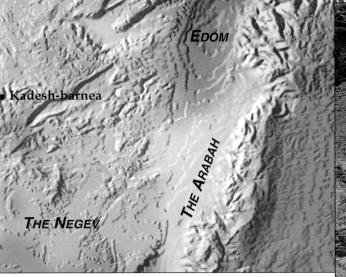

Map: *The region around the Dead Sea.*

"*The glare of Sodom and Gomorrah is flung down the whole length of Scripture history. In this awful hollow, this bit of the infernal regions comes to the surface, this hell with the sun shining into it, primitive man laid the scene of God's most terrible judgment on sin…We feel the flame scorch our own cheeks… Though the glare of this catastrophe burns still, the ruins of it have entirely disappeared, and there remains in the valley no authentic trace of the names it has torn and scattered to infamy across the world.*"

—SIR GEORGE ADAM SMITH

Photo: *The wild Judean wilderness not far from Jericho. The photo is taken from the Essene settlement of Qumran across to the area where the Dead Sea scrolls were discovered. The dark area in the middle foreground is the opening to Cave 4, where the richest find was made.*

The Judean Wilderness

*P*inched between the Judean Highlands and the Dead Sea, just east and southeast of Jerusalem, is the genuine desert land known as the Wilderness of Judea. In the *Moody Bible Atlas*, Barry Beitzel writes: "It is a solitary, howling, rough and rocky wasteland that is nearly devoid of plants and animals and virtually without rainfall." As one ascends from the lush surroundings of Jericho or descends on the backside of Olivet, either way one is shocked at this inhospitable region.

Only then does one catch the full import of David's Psalm 63, written from this very wilderness: "O God, Thou art my God; early will I seek Thee: my soul thirsteth for Thee, my flesh longeth for Thee in a dry and thirsty land, where no water is; to see Thy power and Thy glory, so as I have seen Thee in the sanctuary. Because Thy lovingkindness is better than life, my lips shall praise Thee" (Ps. 63:1-3).

The wilderness plunges in places more than 4,000 feet into the Jordan rift and its ruggedness is accentuated by more than twenty almost impassable gorges carved by seasonal rivers. The land is so desolate that even the bedouin largely leave it alone. Thus it was an ideal location for those who looked for solitude or escape, even though it was near to the key centers in Judea.

David, in his days as a fugitive from Saul, often hid here and in the two desert areas adjoining it to the south: the Wilderness of Ziph (west of Engedi) and the Wilderness of Maon (west of Masada). After debacles at Nob (1 Sam. 21:1-9) and Gath (1 Sam. 21:10), David rallied with his 400 and his family at Adullam. Then, after depositing his family for safe-keeping in Moab, the region from which his great-grandmother came, David seems to have settled at Masada ("the strong hold," see 1 Sam. 22:4).

In defending Keilah from the Philistines, David's whereabouts became known to Saul. The jealous king's relentless pursuit drove David into the wilds, first at the wilderness of Ziph and then the wilderness of Maon (1 Sam. 23:14, 24). Eventually David had to move even deeper into this forbidding territory where he found refuge at the springs of Engedi (where Solomon later planted gardens). After an opportunity to snuff out the life of his pursuer (1 Sam. 24), David returned to the stronghold (Masada?) and penned the haunting words of Psalm 57: "O God, be merciful unto me: for my soul trusteth in Thee: yea, in the shadow of Thy wings will I make my refuge, until these calamities be overpast."

Was it prophetically that David wrote concerning his greater Son when he said: "My soul is among lions: and I lie even among them that are set on fire, even the sons of men, whose teeth are spears and arrows, and their tongue a sharp sword" (Ps. 57:4)? In this very wilderness following His baptism, our Lord faced the ravening lion from hell. After being without provisions for forty days, the Perfect Man proved His impeccability in a three-pronged confrontation with the enemy, triumphing gloriously in it.

John the Baptist, who preached to the multitudes against this barren backdrop, took his sermon from Isaiah 40: "The voice of him that crieth in the wilderness, Prepare ye the way of the Lord, make straight in the desert a highway for our God" (Isa. 40:3). And up through this desert the Saviour came at the end of His ministry as He had at the beginning. Making His way from Jericho, He retraced those early steps as He resolutely marked His pathway to Jerusalem and the cross that awaited Him there.

But Isaiah looked beyond that first coming of Christ to the day when He would return to take up a 1000-year residence on this planet, ruling in splendor from the same city where He was executed in shame. He penned the promise of the Lord concerning the wilderness lands of Israel: "I will open rivers in high places, and fountains in the midst of the valleys: I will make the wilderness a pool of water, and the dry land springs of water" (Isa. 41:18). But was it the longing of Jehovah that His people, desert-dry at their heart, would also turn fruitful in their affections for Him? "That they may see, and know, and consider, and understand together, that the hand of the Lord hath done this, and the Holy One of Israel hath created it" (v. 20). Today we often feel the same—dry as the wilderness in our love for Him, parched and barren in our thought-life. But the day is coming when "...the Lord shall comfort Zion: He will comfort all her waste places; and He will make her wilderness like Eden, and her desert like the garden of the Lord; joy and gladness shall be found therein, thanksgiving, and the voice of melody" (Isa. 51:3).

As the old road from Jerusalem to Jericho twists its torturous way along the rim of Wadi Kelt, the eye is suddenly surprised by St. George's Monastery hugging the cliffside where it can suck some water from springs in the rock.

N Hill Country in the South

o natural landform marks the division between Judea and Samaria. The studied eye notices differences, however, as the Central Ridge Road twists its way south. Samaria has more soil, more rainfall, more vegetation. The ancient terraced hillsides give hint to the once fertile conditions of the region even though much of it now lies dormant because it is part of the contested West Bank.

Judea is not so blessed. The boundary that divides the ancient territory of Judah and Simeon from the other tribal regions began by following the Sorek Valley inland from the coast ten miles south of Joppa. It then bulged northward near Beth-shemesh to include the region given to Benjamin, as far north as Bethel (later lost to the ten tribes of Israel). Following Wadi Makkuk for a short distance, the line then dropped south to follow Wadi Suweinit down to the Jordan River near Jericho.

Because of the slight rainfall in Judea, the region remains largely a plateau, uncut by the furrowed seasonal riverbeds as is true further north. Yet because of the lack of cleared soil (there are rocks everywhere!), very little farming has been attempted in Judah except in the area between Bethlehem and Hebron where the climate is ideal for the famed grapes of Eshcol (from the Hebrew for *cluster of grapes*). Almond blossoms, olives, and figs herald the coming spring on the hillsides toward Jerusalem, and some vegetable farming is done in the valleys with the use of irrigation. Although the land looks unproductive, Abraham was wise in allowing God to choose for him. I have seen at the market in Hebron radishes the size of apples and cabbages twice the size of a man's head. Mamre means *vigorous*, and so it has proven.

This area has produced its hardy crop of vigorous Bible characters as well. It was the giant sons of Anak at Hebron that frightened the Israelites out into the desert the first time they came to Canaan. And when Caleb, who "wholly followed the Lord," was given first choice of any real estate in Eretz Israel, he selected mount Hebron. Why? Joshua 14:12 records his stirring reason: "Now therefore give me this mountain…for thou heardest in that day how the Anakim were there, and that the cities were great and fenced: if so be the Lord will be with me, then I shall be able to drive them out, as the Lord said."

But that was not the beginning of Hebron's Bible history. Abraham had built an altar here (Gen. 13:18) and Sarah died here at 127 years of age (the only woman in the Bible whose age is given at death). For her, Abraham purchased the cave of Machpelah for 400 shekels of silver as a burial ground. (Buried here were Abraham, Sarah, Isaac, Rebekah, Jacob, and Leah; Rachel was buried near Bethlehem, Joseph probably near Shechem.) Isaac was also living here when he died (Gen. 35:27) and from this location Jacob sent Joseph on his fateful search north to find his envious brothers. More than 400 years would transpire before his return trip—in a coffin from Egypt. The Anakim had been squatters there since the patriarchs went down to Egypt and had the audacity to rename it Kiryat Arba, City of the Four, but Caleb and his son-in-law, Othniel, soon made it City of the None. Not a son of Anak was left.

But just when the Lord had given it to Caleb, He asked for it back! Caleb no doubt was willing to allow it to be a city of refuge and a priestly center, but it meant the gates had to be open twenty-four hours—Hebron was vulnerable. So it is in our lives. Having given us new life in Christ, God asks us to give it back to Him. And what for? So that He might use us to provide refuge for those seeking salvation from the avenger, and to give refreshment to the Lord's servants who are weary in His work. Surely Caleb was (and you and I will be) enriched by such an arrangement (see Josh. 20:1-7; 21:11).

Many years later, after the death of Saul, David was anointed king here (2 Sam. 2:4) by the men of Judah, and reigned here for seven-and-a-half years. Here Abner died like a fool, one step from safety, killed by Joab in vengeance for the death of his brother (2 Sam. 3:27). And after David moved his capital to Jerusalem, Absalom campaigned here, stealing the hearts of the men of Israel (2 Sam. 15) in preparation for his coup d'état. Today in Hebron the hearts of the people are just as hotly contested, this being a center of bitter discord between Abram's two sons—militant Moslems and stubborn Jewish settlers.

Two roads joined at Hebron. The trade route from the Nabatean stronghold of Bozrah, southeast of the Dead Sea, ran through Arad to Hebron. The Central Ridge Road rose up from the Negev, then through Beersheba to Hebron. From here the one road traveled along the highlands as far as the Jezreel Valley, stringing the key towns of Israel together like so many pearls. One of these pearls is Bethlehem.

Bethlehem (ancient Ephrath or Ephratah) should not be confused with the city of the same name in Zebulon, about seven miles northwest of Nazareth (*that* would have been an easy journey for that young expectant Nazarene woman!). Bethlehem Judah is four or five miles south of Jerusalem, twelve miles north of Hebron. The town has a long and varied history. It was the home of a false teacher's concubine (Jud. 19:1) in one of the darkest days in Israel's history; it was the home of a false priest (Jud. 17:7-13); and it was the home of a false king—Jeroboam (1 Ki. 11:26). Saul came here after his anointing (1 Sam. 10:2) in search of his father's asses and received news that they had been found, fulfilling Samuel's prophecy concerning him. But his sun was soon to be eclipsed by a young shepherd born here.

In the days of David, Bethlehem was home to some of the stoutest warriors in the realm. Imagine teaching the Shabbat School class with the sons of Jesse, as well as David's nephews—Joab, Abishai, and Asahel (who was buried here after being killed by Abner, 2 Sam. 2:32), and some of those who later became mighty men with David at Adullam—Eleazar and Elhanan (who slew one of Goliath's brothers, 2 Sam. 21:19). This was also the ancestral home of Samuel (1 Sam. 1:1), although he settled in Ramah, just north of Jerusalem, after the ark was taken from Shiloh.

But when all is said and done, Bethlehem is really the story of four boys. Here Rachel died after giving birth to the boy with two names. As her strength ebbed away and she slipped across the Great Divide, she named her boy Ben-oni, son of my sorrow. But Jacob renamed him Benjamin, son of my right hand. So too with our Lord. As far as His deity, He had a Father, but no mother; as to His humanity, He had a mother, but no father. His mother, Mary, saw only as far as the cross, and her heart was pierced through with a sword of sorrow (Lk. 2:35). But the Father saw beyond the cross to the glory. He made Him the Son of His right hand, as expressed in Hebrews 1:3 and 13. Christ is the true Benjamin.

Some generations later, in the bleak period of the Judges already referred to, we have the pathos-filled account of the return of Naomi from Moab, bringing with her Ruth, Moabite widow of one of her deceased sons. How the light breaks through the clouds in this story as the kinsman redeemer, Boaz, not only redeems that which had been lost, but "moreover" asks for Ruth's hand in marriage. The story that commences in a graveyard concludes with a wedding—and the birth of another baby boy. He is named Obed, which has the double meaning of *service* or *worship*, the logical result of the redeemer and redeemed one coming together. The story, of course, does not end there. The unfinished genealogy with which the book ends points to the day when it would be disclosed that this redeemed Gentile not only was accepted into the covenant of promise but was directly related to none other than the Messiah Himself! But then—so am I (see Ruth 1:1; 4:13-22; Mt. 1:5; Eph. 2:11-16; Heb. 2:11-13).

David came from this line. As the third boy in the chain, this shepherd lad—rejected by his brothers and conqueror of the great enemy of the people—was lost to the Gentiles for a while, but eventually became the king. So follows the drama of his greater Son, the Root and Offspring of David.

When at last, as prophesied by Micah (5:2), the Messiah was born here one night, it should have come as no surprise. The Son of My Sorrow; the Kinsman Redeemer; the Shepherd King—where else would you expect Him to be born? Where else had a place been so prepared for Him? Where else would you send the Bread of heaven but to the place called Beit-lehem, the house of bread? Who else would you invite to the celebration but some Gentile wise men who bowed before the All-wise Creator of the stars (Rom. 1:20) and Jewish shepherds to behold the Lamb of God? But now you have been there too, at least in spirit. What is your response? The scholars in Jerusalem could quote the verse (Mt. 2:4-6) but found the four-mile journey too much to endure to find out if it were true. But the unlearned shepherds "made known abroad the saying which was told them concerning this child" (Lk. 2:17). And the wise men? They "fell down, and worshiped Him" (Mt. 2:11).

From the heights of the Herodion, a mountaintop retreat, one of a string of fortifications built by Herod the Great to provide refuge in time of Jewish rebellion against their puppet king. Josephus recorded that Herod was buried here, but no such remains have been found. The town of Bethlehem is in the distance, the town around which Herod sent his soldiers to slaughter the male children under two years, in a satanic attempt to murder the child-king, Jesus. Also nearby is the town of Tekoa, home of the herdsman-prophet, Amos, and of the fabled wise woman referred to in the essay on the following page.

Spilled or Poured?

*I*f you leave Jerusalem by the Jaffa Gate and head south, you will first descend steeply into the head of the Hinnom Valley before rising to the Plain of Rephaim. You may not hear "the sound of a going in the tops of the mulberry trees" but, on a springtime morning or just as evening falls, you'll hear the breeze playing through the almond leaves and hawthorn blossoms and rustling the "tender green" of the fig. The ridge route brings you along the backbone of the Judean high country, five miles southwest to a little town cascading down a double hill. Its inhabitants call it *Beit Lahm*; we know it as Bethlehem.

At Bethlehem, the road branches. The main trade route made its way southwest toward Hebron and Beersheba on the edge of the Negev. A less-traveled road heads straight south and then cuts southeast into the mountains and eventually through the Judean wilderness to the oasis of Engedi on the shores of the Dead Sea. Five miles along that road from Bethlehem is Tekoa or *Khirbet Teku* as it is referred to today.

Circumstances would link these two little Judean towns in the days of David. When the youngest son of Jesse had become the bold chieftan of a band of outlaws and was besieged by the Philistines in the stronghold of Adullam, his heart grew thirsty for a drink from the sweet-watered well of Bethlehem (see 2 Sam. 23:13-17). It was no command he gave, but the outbreathing of his soul. It was, however, enough for three of his mighty men. Slipping out into the darkness, they broke through the enemy lines (you can be sure the water source was "well" protected!) and brought David a dripping skin, filled with the happy memories of a shepherd boy.

The man who would be king was deeply moved. Taking the water bag from the men, he poured it out on the ground. He what? How thoughtless! How wasteful! No, I didn't say he spilled it; he poured it. Knowingly, thoughtfully, worshipfully, David offered it as an irrevocable sacrifice to the Lord. I do not deserve such devotion, he was declaring. But He does. For in that skin, David knew, was the lifeblood of his three valiant men. Nothing would do but that it would be a libation, a drink offering to the Lord.

Thirty-five years roll their course. David, no longer in a cave, lives in a palace. He rules from Eziongeber to the headwaters of the Orontes in Lebanon. But his wayward boys have brought him nothing but grief. He is harvesting a bitter crop from his dark deeds with Bathsheba. His army commander, Joab, privy to the conspiracy against Uriah (2 Sam. 11), now has leverage in the palace. He has found a kindred spirit in Absalom, the wild-hearted son of a Bedouin, whose grandfather was king of Geshur.

Joab has a problem. His compatriot, Absalom, in vengeance on behalf of his sister, slays Amnon, his half-brother, and flees to Geshur. Joab wants him back to strengthen his own hand. In the nearby town of Tekoa there is a "wise woman" who agrees to be Joab's accomplice.

Disguised in mourning apparel, she approaches the king with the sad tale of two sons. With her husband already dead, she says, her one son had killed the other in a fight. As if that wasn't bad enough, now the townspeople want to execute the guilty son for murder. She would have no one left. The climax of her argument is a classic: *"For we must needs die, and are as water spilt on the ground, which cannot be gathered up again"* (2 Sam. 14:14). In other words, Amnon is gone. No use crying over spilled milk, or spilled blood either. Get on with living; we'll all be spilled soon enough.

So who was right? Is it poured or spilled? Is the believer's life haphazardly splashed across the hard ground of circumstance, to be absorbed or evaporated and forgotten? Or are our lives to be a drink offering, poured out as a purposeful act of worship to God?

Paul would side with David, and so would Timothy and Epaphroditus and David's greater Son Himself (Phil. 2). Following the example of the Lord Jesus, the faithful of every age have poured out their lives as servants of Jehovah. We are not spilled by some cosmic accident, to be absorbed by the planet we mistakenly call "Home." May we add our voices to Paul's as he writes to his brothers and sisters: *"If I be offered (poured out as a drink offering) upon the sacrifice and service of your faith, I joy, and rejoice with you all"* (Phil. 2:17).

Jerusalem At Last

We notice the bullet-pocked walls above the Zion Gate as we enter the ancient confines of the Old City. They are a grim reminder that Yerushalayim, the City of Peace, has hardly lived up to its name. These bullet scars were left in 1948, but war is nothing new to this little piece of real estate. About the only times there seem to be any lasting peace associated with it are the days of the king-priest, Melchizedek; the mighty sovereign, Solomon; and the day yet future when these two will find answer in their Antitype, the blessed and only Potentate, the King of kings and Lord of lords who shall rule the world from here. For centuries these lines were reality:

Oh! weep for those that wept by Babel's stream,
Whose shrines are desolate, whose land a dream;
Weep for the harp of Judah's broken shell;
Mourn—where their God had dwelt, the godless dwell.

Tribes of the wandering feet and weary breast,
How shall ye flee away and be at rest?
The wild dove hath her nest, the fox his cave;
Mankind their country, Israel but the grave!

When Lord Byron wrote this dirge, the words were all true, sadly true. But not so today. No longer are Jews forbidden to enter on penalty of death or pay their Gentile rulers for the privilege of weeping at the Wall. Jerusalem is again in the hands of the Jews. For how long? It is hard to see how they would ever give it up until their last drop of blood is spilled in its defense.

Yet we do see—though Israeli soldiers are present—that the great paving stones which once upheld the glorious second temple now display the shrine of the false prophet, Mohammed. Instead of the silver trumpets calling Israel to the house of their God, the muzzein wails for the Moslem faithful to turn their backs on Jerusalem and pray towards Mecca. It is a deeply moving sight to see 10,000 followers of Islam on their faces in prayer on the Temple Mount on the last great day of the fast of Ramadan. Our Saviour is the light for these Gentiles, too.

The Jewish Quarter has been almost completely rebuilt since it was ravaged between 1948 and 1967. But in the rebuilding process, first the layers of previous civilizations were uncovered. So to the careful visitor almost every turn unfolds another time. You can walk along the Cardo, the heart, the main street through Hadrian's Roman city. This was built over the ruins of the city destroyed by Titus, fulfilling the prophecy of the Lord Jesus that the temple would not have one stone left on another. Near the Wall, recent excavations have found the New Testament street that the Lord would have traversed.

You can walk through what is thought to be the high priest's house; look down into the pool of Bethesda with its porticos; linger at the Pavement, the open courtyard of the Antonia fortress where our Lord was put to shame. But you can go back much further than that. See Hezekiah's broad wall defending the vulnerable northern approach and rebuilt by Nehemiah; look down the old Jebusite water shaft through which Joab climbed to deliver the city to David 3,000 years ago; or think long and hard at the heights of Moriah where Abraham offered Isaac and, said the Lord, he "rejoiced to see My day."

You can look down into the Hinnom valley where Manasseh erected an idol to Moloch or up to Ornan's threshing-floor where Solomon built a temple to Jehovah; imagine Isaiah and Hezekiah spreading their need before God or Athaliah defying Him with her slaughter of the seed royal. There is no end to the personalities here as the mind retraces the twisting road from Genesis 15 to Revelation 21.

But they are all gone now. In their place the city streets are filled with multitudes who have never heard that from this very city went forth the Saviour of the world to die for them. Once more we need to heed the Master's plea: "Beginning at Jerusalem…"

Photo: *Across the Kidron to the Old City of Jerusalem (from Olivet). The trees within the wall are on Moriah.*
Inset: *The SE corner of the Temple Mount (also seen in large photo). Perhaps the pinnacle of the temptation.*

George Müller in Jerusalem

During our stay at Jerusalem, we had opportunities also of visiting the various places of interest for which the city is celebrated. The Via Dolorosa, the Mosque of Omar (built on the site formerly occupied by Solomon's Temple), the Church of the Holy Sepulcher (erected, according to tradition, on the spot where our Lord was crucified), Absalom's Pillar, the Pool of Bethesda, the site of Herod's palace, the ruins of the Castle to which Paul was taken, and the pool of Siloam, were all visited in turn. One of the most memorable places in the city is "The Wailing Place of the Jews" where, every Friday afternoon, shortly before sunset, they assemble to bewail the calamities that have befallen their land and city. On Dec. 2 we saw about 200 Israelites gathered close to some immense old stones, the remains of the Temple it is supposed, which, after praying and bowing repeatedly, with tears in their eyes, they kissed.

In the streets of Jerusalem, day after day, we saw numbers of men, women and children standing about half-naked, or clothed in miserable rags; and strangers cannot walk a short distance even, without being besieged for alms by the beggars that abound, not a few of whom are lepers. They hold up their disfigured hands and arms, and, pointing to their dreadful sores, follow visitors persistently, entreating them, in piteous, lamentable tones of voice, to have compassion on, and to help them.

Whilst at Jerusalem, from the windows of our room, we saw many funeral processions pass, when the remains of the deceased were borne along, either in open coffins, or in coffins with glass covers to them; and on Dec. 23 the funeral of a child, belonging to the Greek Church, took place outside the city walls, whose body was lowered into the grave without a coffin.

As there are no carriage roads in Palestine, with the exception of the one from Jaffa to Jerusalem, being unwilling to undertake long journeys of many miles on horseback, in order to visit the numerous places of interest usually resorted to by strangers, we did not travel any further into the interior of the country; but, after remaining at Jerusalem for nine weeks and two days, on Feb. 1, 1882, returned to Jaffa. There, heavy gales of wind and violent storms of rain, which lasted several days, detained us until Feb. 8th; the weather became also unusually cold, and as there were neither stoves nor fireplaces in the rooms of our hotel, because fires are seldom wanted in Palestine, we suffered greatly from the wintry climate.

During this our second visit to Jaffa, Mr. Müller again held meetings for the Germans; and on Wednesday, Feb. 8th, the violence of the gales having to some extent abated, we embarked for Haipha (Haifa) on the coast of Palestine, about 70 miles north of Jaffa. Our passage, however, in a small boat, to the Austrian steamship, "Flora," lying at a considerable distance from the shore, during weather still tempestuous, was most trying and even dangerous; for, after sailing over heavy breakers, and getting clear of the rocks, our boat was tossed about upon the waves for nearly half an hour; and, after at last we reached the ship, a favourable opportunity of getting a footing on board, to be seized just at the right moment as the boat was lifted upwards by the waves, had to be closely watched for, when one after the other, at the risk of our lives, we had to spring on to the steep ladder staircase that led up towards the deck.

At 2 o'clock the vessel sailed, and on the evening of that day, at half-past 9, we arrived off Haipha, where, in consequence of the roughness of the sea, and our distance from the shore, it became a question whether we should disembark at all; but after considering the matter, and praying over it, we resolved to brave the disagreeables and land. Some time elapsed before the boat, which had been sent ashore with passengers, returned; but soon after midnight, with less discomfort than had been experienced at Jaffa, we were rowed safely to the beach. There, some German brethren were waiting our arrival with an open wagon, in which, during torrents of rain, we were conveyed to the Hotel du Mont Carmel, a mile and a half distant, where we arrived soon after 1 o'clock.

—Mrs. Susannah Müller in *The Preaching Tours and Missionary Labours of George Müller*, recounting a tour taken of Egypt, Palestine, Syria, Asia Minor, Turkey, and Greece from August 23, 1881 to May 30, 1882, pp. 180-183

The Name

*A*s you enter the Old City of Jerusalem by way of the Zion Gate, you may notice an inscription, written in the days of Suleiman, stating that the gate was constructed in 1541 AD. The wall here is pocked with gunfire. During the fiery rebirth of Israel in 1948, the Jewish Palmach breached the gate for a short time and secured a passage into the besieged Jewish Quarter before being forced to withdraw. It was not until 1967 that the Israeli Defense Forces broke into the Old City again, through the Lion's Gate and this Zion Gate to secure the Temple Mount.

Only the Zion Gate—and the Dung Gate, further east along the southern wall—allows direct entrance into the Jewish Quarter. We step, for a moment, out of the brilliant sunshine into the deep shadow under the crenelated walls of Old Salem. If we have not been blinded by the sudden change of lighting, or distracted by trying to avoid a vehicle twisting its way through the narrow passage we are sharing with it, we might notice a cylindrical object fastened to the wall. It is a large *mezuzah*, similar to ones found on the doorposts of faithful Jewish households.

The word *mezuzah* is simply the Hebrew for "doorpost" and is the name given to the container for a parchment scroll inscribed with Deuteronomy 6:4-9 and 11:13-21. It also includes the name of God, Shaddai. If we stand and watch for a minute, we might see orthodox Jews, dressed in black, side locks dancing in the breeze, hurrying by. Often they will brush their fingertips across their lips and then across the *mezuzah* at the gate. It is to them, perhaps, a sign of respect or affection, or a "sacred" good luck charm. But one cannot help but wonder if this is a classic expression of "lip service" to the Lord while their hearts are far from Him (see Isa. 29:13; Mk. 7:6).

Jews faithful to their religion will not use the name of God. His covenant name, Yahweh, or YHWH, must never be spoken; it is too holy, they say. In fact, even government brochures, if they must speak of the Deity, spell it G_d. Instead, He is often referred to simply as *la shem*, the Name. This usage is quite biblical. Often "the name of God" is used to speak of God Himself. To "call upon the name of the Lord" was to express dependence on Him; to "forget His name" was to turn away from a relationship with Him; to "take the name of the Lord in vain" was to, at the same time, acknowledge Him (by using His name) and deny Him (by abusing it).

The name of the Lord that the Jews will use (as on the mazuzot) is the mighty-tender name of El Shaddai, the God of power (El) and provision (Shaddai, from *shad*, the breast). It is the name that links most closely the fatherly authority and motherly affection of God. The name begins with the Hebrew letter *Schin*—pronounced sheen (you might find one in your Bible at Psalm 119, above verse 161).

The present inhabitants of Jerusalem are glad to explain that, from the air (or heaven, if you will), the mountain-valley topography around their capital city forms this letter. The left branch and base follow the path of the Hinnom Valley around the west and south flanks of Mount Zion; the central branch can be superimposed upon the Tyropean Valley which separates Mount Zion from Moriah; and the right branch of the Schin takes the route of the Kidron Valley between Moriah on the west and Olivet on the east. Thus they quote Psalm 125:2, "As the mountains are round about Jerusalem, so the Lord is round about His people from henceforth even forever."

In the New Testament, the name of the Lord Jesus is invested with everything included in the "name of God" in the Old Testament. Sinners are saved through believing on His name (Jn. 1:12; 2:23). All who are, should be baptized in that name and begin to gather with the Lord's people, meeting in that name. We are to "pray" and "ask" in that name (Jn. 14:13-14; 15:16; 16:23-24). This would bring the animosity of the world, the Lord said, and we would be hated for His name's sake.

And so it came to pass. Peter and John were forbidden to "speak at all or teach in the name of Jesus" (Acts 4:18). Again they said, "Did we not straightly command you that ye should not teach in this name?" Beaten and expelled, they departed, "rejoicing that they were counted worthy to suffer shame for His name." Do we?

I Know Where the Ark Is!

*I*n February of 1989, a modest second-floor apartment in the Jewish Quarter of the old city of Jerusalem opened its doors to the public. Hugging the eastern slope of Mount Zion, its windows look expectantly toward the rugged southern brow of Moriah.

Here is the Temple Institute, founded in 1988 by Rabbi Israel Ariel with the following objectives: to encourage, synthesize, and house research on the temples of Judaism; to prepare the holy vessels for the coming temple; and to educate and stimulate world Jewry in anticipation of the temple becoming again the focus of their national and religious life. How are they doing?

At present, in conjunction with the Ministry of Religious Affairs, the Temple Institute has sponsored conferences on temple research, bringing together rabbis, archaeologists, gemologists, architects, and various scientists and craftsmen to share information on the project. More than half of the 103 vessels are already made, including containers for the blood, silver trumpets, a copper laver, the golden censer, and some of the priestly garments. Books have been published, videos distributed, and both permanent and traveling displays spread the word. Money is being collected. (The golden menorah, requiring almost 100 pounds of the precious metal, is estimated to cost $10 million!) Are they serious? Very serious.

I was sitting with a group of Christians in a small amphitheater at the Institute this past May. After the lecture, the rabbi opened the floor for questions.

What were they going to do, someone wanted to know, about the missing ark of the covenant.

"It's not missing," responded the rabbi assuredly, "we know exactly where it is. When the time comes, we'll bring it out."

There were other questions, and then the dialogue went something like this:

"When I read the Hebrew Scriptures, I notice a great deal about the blood. Do you have any blood sacrifices today?"

"No," responded the rabbi somewhat edgily, "but the use of blood sacrifices was only one way for redemption. For example, there was the redemption money."

"Yes," came the answer softly, "but even then it was not without blood. Does your Scripture not say, 'Without the shedding of blood is no remission' ?"

At this point, it was obvious that the dialogue was deteriorating into a diatribe. The temperature in the room suddenly warmed. "I know what you're getting at," came the shrill rejoinder, "and when I think of Him I see red, alright! But it's not His blood; it's the blood of millions of Jews murdered in His name. So let's drop the subject (this through his teeth) and keep the conversation friendly."

Actually the conversation was over. The rabbi had seen to that. He had let us know in no uncertain terms that one Subject was off-limits there. We could talk about the linen being carefully woven for the priests yet to be, but we could not mention our sympathetic Great High Priest (Heb. 4:14-16). We could examine the model of the candlestick, but we must not allude to the One who was the Light of the world (Jn. 8:12). We were welcome to ask questions about the red heifer, but not the Lamb of God (Jn. 1:29). And we could discuss the location of the ark of the covenant—was it destroyed by Nebuchadnezzar in the sixth century BC, is it in Ethiopia somewhere, or is it under the temple mount in a sealed passageway awaiting the day of the dedication of the new temple? But don't talk about the One "whom God hath set forth to be a propitiation through faith in His blood…that He might be just, and the justifier of him which believeth in Jesus" (Rom. 3:25-26). Who knows where you might end up?

There. I've let the secret out. I know where the Ark is. The little gold box built by Aholiab and Bezaleel was only a figure of the true (Heb. 9:24). Our Lord does not fit well into a box. His glory, which once filled the Holiest, now fills the heavens.

The transported ark once caught the eye of the pilgrim Israelite with its covering of blue as they wended their way through the wilderness. On our desert journey through this world's wasteland, there is one truth that quickens our step and strengthens our heart. We know what's beyond the blue.

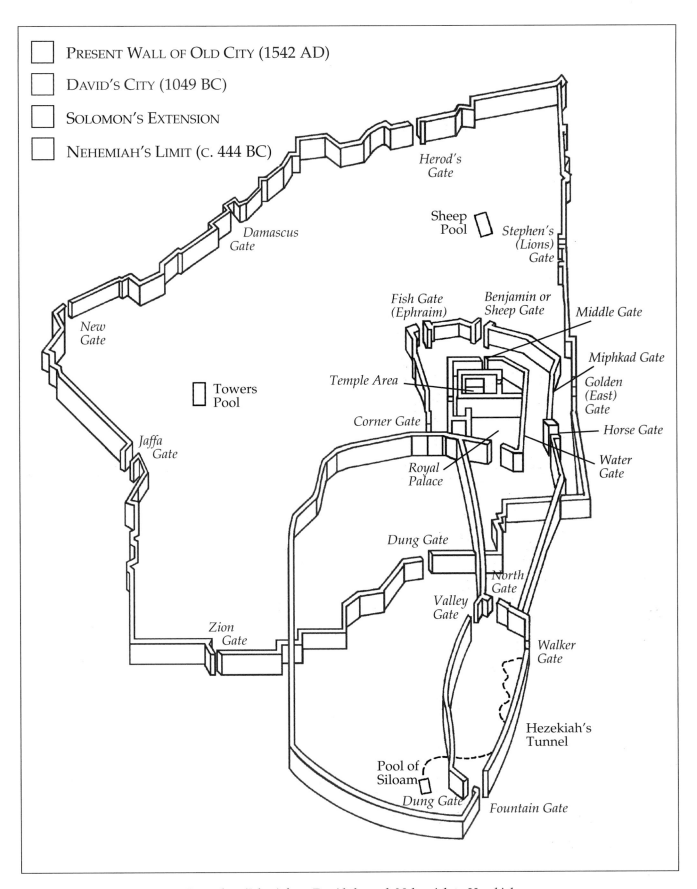

PRESENT WALL OF OLD CITY (1542 AD)

DAVID'S CITY (1049 BC)

SOLOMON'S EXTENSION

NEHEMIAH'S LIMIT (C. 444 BC)

Herod's Gate

Sheep Pool

Stephen's (Lions) Gate

Damascus Gate

New Gate

Fish Gate (Ephraim)

Benjamin or Sheep Gate

Middle Gate

Miphkad Gate

Golden (East) Gate

Temple Area

Corner Gate

Horse Gate

Towers Pool

Royal Palace

Water Gate

Jaffa Gate

Dung Gate

North Gate

Valley Gate

Walker Gate

Zion Gate

Hezekiah's Tunnel

Pool of Siloam

Dung Gate

Fountain Gate

Jerusalem (Jebus) from David through Nehemiah to Hezekiah

71

How many thousands of prayers, how many millions of tears have poured forth from Jewish hearts at the Wall!
An ultra-orthodox Jew adds his petitions to those of his brethren, perhaps including a call for the coming of Messiah.

Up Against the Wall

*I*t is an irony that should not be missed: the true symbol of Judaism is a wall. The country's department of tourism uses a rendition of two spies carrying a cluster of Eschol's grapes; the Israeli flag is emblazoned with *magen David*, the six-pointed shield; the knesset (parliament) boasts a large seven-branched menorah. But world Jewry always finds its way to the Wall.

The Wall, or *ha-Kotel*, is often called by Gentiles the Wailing Wall—never by the Jews; they call it *Kotel Ha'Maaravi* or the Western Wall). It is really a portion of the Herodian retaining wall built to enlarge the Temple Mount area. Mount Moriah's southern peak was not large enough for Herod the Great's grandiose plans, so he had a large stone "table" built over the summit. The outer (eastern) wall of the city was extended to the south, and three other walls were built in a rough rectangle around the base of the mountain. Then, upheld by pillars, domes, and arches, a huge platform was built between the walls (approx. 1000 ft. x 1500 ft.). On this expansive tabletop were erected the temple precincts. Herod beautified the Second Temple, including the addition of a solid gold crown around its parapet.

Sitting on the commanding slope of Olivet east of the city, a knot of men gathered around a Prophet, circa AD 29. They were impressed with Herod's beautification program in the Eternal City. But their Master told them, "There shall not be left here one stone upon another" (Mt. 24:2). Could it be?

One generation would pass. This last great Prophet, the Stone rejected by the builders, would be executed outside the city walls. The fledgling Church would be scattered by the threatenings and slaughter of one, Saul of Tarsus. Israel, chafing under the Roman yoke, in 66 AD rebelled against her masters, bringing down the fury of Titus and his Legionnaires. After a bloody five-year siege, the city was put to the torch. And the temple's golden crown, once her glory, would bring about her final shame. Running down between her mighty stones, its wealth, once cooled, was sought by the soldiers by breaking each stone apart. All that was left was the Wall. The first few layers on top were thrown over into the valley, but the work became more difficult with succeeding rows. The stones each weigh several tons (one stone north of the plaza approximates 400 tons!) The Romans left off their destruction and so the Wall remains.

Half a world away, in Richmond, British Columbia, I was standing in a print shop, waiting to have a chart copied. In came a cheerful woman, dark haired, sallow skinned. She greeted the proprietor and then stood beside me, waiting to be served. She noticed my chart. "Is that yours?" she asked. I nodded.

"What is it about?"

"These are the major teachings of the Bible."

"Would you explain it to me?"

The conversation lasted an hour-and-a-half. She kept coming back to the Jews. Why? I asked her.

"I'm a Jew," she said. "I just arrived from Israel."

The conversation took a turn at that point and we made progress until she asked, "Do I have to become a religious Jew to make it to heaven?" (Heaven? Had she been peeking at the New Testament?)

I told her I didn't know any religious Jews. There were many in Israel, she said. I said I had never met a religious Jew, even among the ultra-orthodox. Puzzled, she asked me what I meant.

"You know the Jewish religion, don't you? The true God lives in the Holiness of Holinesses. Outside are the sinners—all of us. In between is an altar, and a priest, and a sacrifice. Your scripture says, 'Without shedding of blood is no remission.' Do these religious Jews have an altar? A priest? A lamb?"

Her hopeless countenance gave me her answer.

"Your scriptures give the solution. Isaiah said that Messiah would be 'wounded for our transgressions.' God would lay on Him our iniquity"…

It was then that she came to the Wall. I saw it in her eyes. After a few more words to her about what Yeshua meant to me, and encouraging her to examine the New Testament, written by Jews who took their prophets seriously, she left the shop. My prayers followed her out the door. They follow her still. Because I know Someone who can take down walls more mighty than *Kotel Ha'Maaravi* (Eph. 2:14).

The Long Wait

For the last nineteen centuries the cry, "Ad mosai?" ("Until when?") has risen from the hearts of expectant Jews everywhere. Since the Carpenter Yeshua from Nazareth was rejected by the nation of Israel, others have risen to claim the role. The most notable include Bar-Kochba, who led the bloody Great Revolt against the Romans in 132-135 AD, and Shabbetai Zevi in the seventeenth century. Recently the Lubavitcher Rebbe Mendel Menachem Schneerson of Brooklyn, New York, has been heralded as *Moshiach.*

Born in Russia in 1902, Schneerson was immersed by his father in the Jewish religion. By *bar mitzvah* age, he was considered a Torah prodigy. After studying at the Sorbonne in Paris, he settled in the U.S. in 1941 and at age 48, assumed leadership of the Habad or Lubavitcher movement.

The Habad movement, with headquarters in Brooklyn, is active throughout the world. More than a quarter of a million children are taught in Lubavitcher (after a town in Bylorussia where the movement had its roots) schools. One of the fundamental tenets of this movement is the belief that in every genera- tion there is a "potential Messiah." In this generation, they believed, the potential Messiah was Menachem Schneerson. Although Schneerson gave halfhearted denials, he did little to discourage his fol- lowers from promoting his claims. "I'm not saying he is or isn't Moshiach," said Rabbi Chayim Bergstein in the *Detroit Jewish News* (Jan. 3/92), "but there is no one as learned, as pious, as caring, as courageous, as intellectual and as influential in this generation. These are all the traits Maimonides identified as belonging to Moshiach."

"Rabbi Schneerson is the Messiah. I don't have to think twice about it," said a Jewish woman inter- viewed by an *Associated Press* reporter. "We talk about it a lot and we are waiting for the big event."

In an expensive campaign to crown Menachem Schneerson as Messiah, more than 200 billboards were installed and full-page advertisements shouted: "Moshiach is coming and we must make final preparations." May of 1992 saw a "Moshiach Parade" down Fifth Avenue in Manhattan with tens of thousands cheering. And this in spite of the fact that the rabbi had suffered a stroke the previous March and was now past ninety. In fact, as his health waned, it seemed the frenzy grew. As 1993 drew to a close, a *Jewish Telegraph Agency* release stated: "The Lubavitcher Rebbe's health has deteriorated to the point where he is almost completely blinded by cataracts, has lost physical mobility and is a virtual pris- oner in his own room…"

Undeterred, his followers placed ads like this in the January 29/94 *Jerusalem Post*, reading, "The Lubavitcher Rebbe Menachem M. Schneerson is the King Moshiach. Now is the time to accept his king- ship!" Then Schneerson suffered another stroke. On Sunday, June 12, 1994, he died.

What happens when your Messiah dies? Some of his followers simply denied the reports of his death: "He's the Messiah. He's not dead." Others flew to New York, hoping "they could be present when Rabbi Schneerson would somehow proclaim his kingship before being buried." Hope dies a hard death.

What happens when your Messiah dies? Ask the two on the Emmaus road (Lk. 24:13-35). The long wait (20 centuries!) since the Seed was promised had been rewarded with a Man that not only *claimed* to be Moshiach but *proved* it. Now He was dead. Or so they thought until "Jesus Himself drew near…"

Was Schneerson born in Bethlehem (Micah 5:2)? Did Bar Kokhba avoid the curse on Jechoniah by being virgin-born (Isa. 7:14)? Did Shabbetai Zevi die the death prophesied in Psalm 22 and Isaiah 53? Could any of them ask: "Which of you convinces me of sin?" Could they raise the dead—or for that mat- ter, rise again themselves? Don't get me wrong. The Jews are right in waiting for Messiah. He will come. The long wait will be rewarded. However, Anti-messiah will first present his credentials. Many will be deluded. But when there is no place left to turn, and Israel's little remnant at last looks up, He will come. "We knew it," they will say. "But…these wounds!" (see Isaiah 53:5).

Ah, He was wounded for *our* transgressions. The Lamb! God's Lamb! At last, it will all make sense. Come, Moshiach!

Is Jesus Really the Promised Messiah?

*I*t wasn't my idea! Isaiah, the Hebrew seer, unabashedly declares: "Unto us a child is born, unto us a son is given: and the government shall be upon His shoulder: and His name shall be called Wonderful, Counselor, the mighty God, the everlasting Father, the Prince of Peace. Of the increase of His government and peace there shall be no end, upon the throne of David…even forever" (Isa. 9:6-7). Such a shocking statement to a Jew, linking the ideas of a child being born and His name being the mighty God!

Recently, while having dinner at a hotel in Jerusalem, I quoted this verse to a Jewish doctor who was sharing our table. Her response: "That's isn't in *our* Bible, is it?" She was even more confounded when I quoted from Genesis 1: "In the beginning God (plural) created (singular) the heaven and the earth…and *God* said, Let *us* make man in *our* image" (1:1, 26). She was absolutely non-plussed when I quoted Proverbs 30:4, "Who hath ascended up into heaven, or descended? who hath gathered the wind in His fists?…[God, of course!] what is His name, *and what is His Son's name,* if thou canst tell?"

It has been hotly denied by the Jewish people generally that Jesus of Nazareth is the promised Messiah. But it is now also denied by many Jews that a real, literal, human Messiah is even *promised* in the Bible. It is, they say, an idea imposed by Christians on their Scriptures. But this could not be. The hope of the Messiah has been held by Jews since first the promises began to be made four millennia ago.

Nor was this denial of a personal Messiah, with few exceptions, the conviction of the great rabbinical scholars. The Talmud* declares that "all the prophets have only prophesied concerning the days of the Messiah" (*Sanhedrin* 34, col. 2). Do the Targums deny the coming Messiah? No, writes David Baron, "they are *intensely* messianic, and many a passage is, in their versions, applied to the Messiah in which even Christians fail to see the reference." He adds that there are no less than 72 passages in the Hebrew Scriptures which the Targumim attribute directly to the mention of the Messiah. Maimonides, strong antagonist of Christianity, composed this article of the Jewish creed: "I believe with a perfect faith that the Messiah will come, and although His coming be delayed, I will await His daily appearance." Aben Ezra, Rashi, and Kimchi all add their voices in approval. Don Isaac Ben Yehudah (called Abravanel or Abarbanel), in his commentary on Exodus 22:20, writes: "We ought to remember the redemption and love of God, and to pray to Him in accordance with what was announced by every prophet from Moses (peace be upon him!) to Malachi (peace be upon him!). Whoever doubts that [Messiah will come] makes the law to lie,…and denies God and the words of His prophets" (1881 edition, p. 8).

Of course, showing that a personal Messiah has always been the Bible-based hope of the Jews in no way shows that the messianic prophecies find their fulfillment in the one called Jesus of Nazareth. Judaism at the time of Jesus was sharply divided. Of course the early church was almost entirely composed of Jews, Jews who were convinced that Jesus qualified on every point of the messianic promises. Those convinced included members of the Jewish high court, many priests, even Saul of Tarsus who had been hand-picked to eradicate this sect of Jesus-followers. The Christian New Testament was written overwhelmingly if not completely by Jews. The church's first preachers—and martyrs—were all Jews.

The standard set by God to authenticate His prophecies was extreme; they must be 100% correct. "The prophet, which shall presume to speak a word in My name, which I have not commanded him to speak…even that prophet shall die. And if thou say in thine heart, How shall we know the word which the Lord hath not spoken? When a prophet speaketh in the name of the Lord, if the thing follow not, nor come to pass, that is the thing which the Lord hath not spoken…" (Deut. 18:20-22).

Even Josephus gave some credence to Jesus' Messiahship. Professor Schlomo Pines of the Hebrew University, Jerusalem, translated the following from an Arabic manuscript (it is thought the original text

---

* Jewish oral tradition was organized by Rabbi Akiba (d. 135 AD), revised by Rabbi Meir, and completed about 200 AD by Judah, great-grandson of Hillel. This is known as the Mishnah. Commentary on the Mishnah was called the Gemaras. The combination of the Mishnah and the Gemaras form the Talmud (F. F. Bruce). The Torah (Pentateuch) which God gave takes 350 pages; man's commentary takes up 523 *books* printed in 22 volumes (J. Phillips).

We look down into the Pool of Bethesda. It was a double pool, one for preparing the sacrificial animals for the temple just to the south; the other, the gathering place of the infirm, where our Lord healed a man who had lain there for 38 years.

was corrupted) of Josephus' *Antiquities* (18:3), "At this time there was a wise man who was called Jesus. And his conduct was good and [he] was known to be virtuous. And many people from among the Jews and other nations became his disciples. Pilate condemned him to be crucified and to die. And those who had become his disciples did not abandon his discipleship. They reported that he had appeared to them three days after his crucifixion and that he was alive; accordingly, he was perhaps the messiah concerning whom the prophets have recounted wonders." Perhaps?

What kind of fulfilled prophecies do Christians put forward to verify their claim that Jesus is the Messiah? After all, don't others claim similar predictions for Nostradamus, Mother Shipton, Edgar Cayce, and Jeane Dixon? Anyone who has read the nebulous prognostications of the above, open to an array of meanings, a few of which were "fulfilled" only in a general way, would never compare them with the clear statements of the Hebrew prophets. Isaiah 46:9-10 records: "I am God, and there is none like Me, declaring the end from the beginning, and from ancient times the things that are not yet done."

Obviously in such short scope it is not possible to even cite, let alone discuss, the hundreds of statements concerning Messiah in the Hebrew Scriptures. There are more than 90 prophecies specifically quoted by New Testament writers in a messianic sense. I mention a few, but they give more than enough evidence to convince the seeker for truth. Remember that such evidence convinced thousands, not at first pantheistic Greeks and Romans, but monotheistic Jews (who continued in their monotheism, by the way). And whatever else is said of Rabbi Jesus, never forget that He has convinced more animists, atheists, materialists, and religionists around the world to worship the true God—the God of Abraham—than all the other rabbis together! Former cannibals in Irian Jaya, pygmies in Africa's Ituri Forest, prisoners in Siberian prison camps, and millions more, would tell you that Jesus Christ is worth living—and dying—for. Few Jews worship their Jehovah, but multitudes of *goyim* do, and all because of Jesus.

Did you know that the Hebrew Scriptures carefully detail the family through which, and birthplace to which, the Messiah would come? Notice how the successive prophecies narrow the field of possibilities. It was declared that the Promised Deliverer would be in the human family (Gen. 3:15); through the line of Shem (a Semite, Gen. 9:26); of the seed of Abraham (Gen. 22:18); through Isaac, not Ishmael (Gen. 26:4); and by Jacob, not Esau (Gen. 28:14); in the tribe of Judah, not from the other eleven (Gen. 49:10); and from the family of David (2 Sam. 7:12-16). Isaiah 7:14 states He must be virgin born (to avoid the curse on Jeconiah, or Coniah, see Jer. 22:24-30 & Mt. 1:11-16 for Joseph's line); and Micah 5:2 pinpoints His birthplace at Bethlehem (the rabbis knew that was Messiah's birthplace, see Mt. 2:4-6). For those who wish to take the time, Daniel prophesies the 483 years from the decree to rebuild the temple (Neh. 2:1-8) until Messiah would come "to make reconciliation for iniquity, and to bring in everlasting righteousness …And after threescore and two weeks shall Messiah be cut off, but not for Himself" (see Dan. 9:24-26).

This "cutting off" is the subject of most of the messianic prophecies, including the price paid for His betrayal: "Give me My price;…So they weighed for My price thirty pieces of silver…And I took the thirty pieces of silver, and cast them to the potter in the house of the Lord (Zech. 11:12-13). Note also these details: the piercing of His side (Zech. 12:10); the vinegar offered to Him (Ps. 69:21); the unnatural darkness, the mocking, the nakedness, gambling for His clothes, His great cry, and His piercing (Ps. 22).

Is there hope for those who discover their guilt in the rejection of God's Messiah? For make no mistake, it is *the whole human race* that stands condemned at the cross. It was because of what we were and what we had done that He died. Listen to Zechariah 12:10, 13:1, "I will pour upon the house of David, and upon the inhabitants of Jerusalem, the spirit of grace and of supplications: and they shall look upon Me whom they have pierced, and they shall mourn for Him, as one mourneth for his only son…In that day there shall be a fountain opened…for sin and for uncleanness." Is it for Jews only? No, because when "He came unto His own, and His own received Him not…as many as received Him, to them gave He power to become the sons of God, even to them that believe on His name" (Jn. 1:11-12).

Moody at Gordon's Calvary

Mr. Moody was incredulous on all the traditional sights seen in Jerusalem except the Temple and Calvary. He said that most of the localities were obscure, "but the hills you cannot change or remove." Mr. George D. Mackay, of New York, who joined the party on the trip, says of this first day in the Holy city: "Our walk around Zion Hill finished at the Joppa Gate. Just before reaching it we saw a group of lepers. The sight was pitiful in the extreme. The thought of contamination was uppermost, and we hurried by, anxious to pass such misery. In the afternoon, Paul, Donald [Mr. Mackay's son], and I got donkeys and rode to the top of the Mount of Olives. On the way we passed Calvary."

Mr. Moody took his Bible early Easter morning and went to the Mount of Olives. In the afternoon he preached to a large audience on Calvary under the auspices of the English Church Missionary Society. At least three hundred people were present, largely native and visiting Christians. Some Mussulmans (Moslems) and Jews came to listen, attracted by the crowd. Mr. Moody was in excellent spirits and preached with an emotion that he had rarely, if ever, equalled in any previous sermon. He hardly chose a text, beginning by saying that he had preached for thirty years, but had never felt the awe of God that he did at that moment.

He pointed out the various spots in sight and linked them with their stories in the Bible—Mizpah and Samuel, Moriah and Abraham, the distant hills of Moab and Ruth, Olivet and Jesus. He likened the sacrifice of Isaac to the coming offering up of Jesus,

D. L. Moody preaching at Gordon's Calvary on Easter Sunday, 1893

and spoke of how Jesus must have felt as He passed this hill in His boyhood, knowing that there He should offer up His life. He spoke of the feasts that Jesus had attended on yonder temple site, and how the burden of His preaching at each one was the new birth in the power of the Spirit...The sermon was preached with a fervor beyond description, and left an ineffaceable impression on all who heard it.

P.S. The Moslems later objected to Mr. Moody preaching from a tombstone in their cemetery. Moody's reply: "I don't blame them. I wouldn't want any man to stand on my father's grave to preach either!" The cemetery was so dilapidated at that time it was assumed to be deserted, which in fact it was.

—from W. R. Moody's *The Life of Dwight L. Moody by His Son*, describing the tour of Palestine he shared with Moody in April of 1893, pp. 384-385. Moody had been asked to go earlier in the previous year, but was occupied with gospel work in Scotland, being left alone there as Mr. Sankey was in London to attend C. H. Spurgeon's funeral (from a letter dated February 10, 1892).

Where is Calvary?

*T*here has been considerable debate over the years concerning the actual site of Golgotha, Skull Hill. It would seem that the Lord, knowing the tendency of the human heart to adore just about anything but what it should rightly adore, has kept its location uncertain.

The traditional site, which various religious groups use to their monetary advantage, is located in the "Church of the Holy Sepulcher." This property was purchased by Helena, mother of Constantine, in 335 AD. Those who hold to this location have yet to prove the following to my satisfaction:

1. That it was outside the city wall. In order for their theory to work, the wall must make an elbow inward, weakening the defense and following an unlikely topography, skirting the Tyropean Valley instead of keeping the high ground, from which the enemy would find it easy to attack the city.

2. That in fulfillment of the Levitical requirement, the Great Sacrifice was offered on the north side of the altar. In fact, the Church of the Holy Sepulcher site is almost straight *west* of the temple, whereas the so-called Gordon's Calvary is on the north.

3. That in fulfillment of Genesis 22, "in the mount of the Lord"—Mount Moriah—it was to be seen. Surely it was no accident that the Lord brought Abraham past a score of mountains to this one. The Church of the Holy Sepulcher is not on Moriah, but the skull-shaped hill outside the Damascus Gate is. In fact, Moriah is a ridge with three peaks: the southern peak (the threshing-floor of Ornan) where the temple was built for the Jews, and where the Dome of the Rock now stands; the central peak, where the Antonia fortress was built for the Romans; and the northern peak, where the Jews and the Romans united to execute the Son of God. But *we* were there, too. We were all there. The whole universe was gathered there that day—Jews and Gentiles, angels and demons, God and the arch-fiend. And in the midst, that solitary Figure on which your eternity and mine hung. "There they crucified Him."

Likely the drama of Genesis 22 did not occur at the place where, a thousand years later, the temple would be built. It seems to me more likely that the sacrifice of Isaac took place at the north end of the mountain, away from the peering eyes of the inhabitants of Salem where Melchizedek was king.

You would expect a grateful father to call the place "The Lord *has* provided." But Abraham rejoiced to see Messiah's day, and called it "The Lord *will* provide." How appropriate then that the Father and the Son should go "both of them together" up the same hill.

4. That any major thoroughfare passed by the traditional site. To points west, the road left the city by the Jaffa Gate hard by Herod's palace and traversed the north end of the Hinnom Valley before crossing the foothills into the Aijalon Valley that led to the coast. To points north, the Nablus Road left by the Damascus Gate and passed by the Skull (referred to in Jewish tradition as the city's place of execution).

For those who have been there and compared the sites, J. Howard Kitchen says it well: "Many visitors naturally revere the Church of the Holy Sepulcher as the traditional site…Others will generally turn with some relief from this dark, forbidding pile of buildings, hung with countless lamps, crowded with sacred sites, and heavy with incense, to that hill outside the city wall, and to the tomb in the garden where there is no dome but the blue sky, and no music but the song of birds and the sound of the wind in the trees."

The geographical spot may be uncertain, but there is one thing that is sure. Calvary is man's only hope. And God has seen to it that no pilgrimage is needed to this place; it is as close as a prayer, a heart's breadth away. Evangeline Booth wrote, "I have seen men find Him where the shepherds did—in a barn; where Paul did—on a journey; where Mary of Magdala did—in a garden; where the jailer did—in a prison. I have seen men find Him on the seas, in the forests, down in the mines, and in the most evil places outside of hell. I saw a man find Him on his knees in a tavern, with his head on the bar over which he had bartered all his life's happiness. There is no spot on earth where Christ will not come to meet us if we will only seek Him with a heart that so thirsts it will go to any length to find Him."

Where is Calvary? Wherever a sinner meets his Saviour; wherever a believer meets his Beloved. The place may be forgotten; it is the Person we need.

Photo: *Calvary, the northern peak of Mount Moriah.*
Inset: *The Garden Tomb at the base of Calvary.*

I Watched a Lamb Die

*U*ntil recently, just outside the Lion's Gate, hugging the eastern wall of the old city of Jerusalem was the last vestige of what was once a thriving sheep market. In Bible times, Jews scattered through the ancient world by various *diasporas* would make their way home to worship in the City of the Name. But no man ever came to God aright without a substitutionary sacrifice. Of course it was impossible to bring your own lamb on the long journey to Israel. Therefore the need for a supply near at hand was satisfied by this market by the wall.

Just in through the Lion's Gate and to the right lie the ruins of the double pool called Bethesda (house of mercy). Some of its porticos can still be seen. One pool was for humans but the other was for animals. Being washed here and checked for blemishes, the still living sacrifices were then taken in through the Sheep Gate on the northern wall of the temple enclosure. There, on the elevation of Moriah's southern peak, "before the Lord" the lamb would die.

Early one morning in May, I slipped out of my hotel overlooking the Hinnom Valley. It was still dark. I hailed a taxi and headed for the sheep market. Down into the valley past the Sultan's Pool. Up the other side and along the edge of Mount Zion. Past the Jaffa Gate and around the northwest corner of the Old City. Along the northern wall past the New, Damascus, and Herod's Gates. Through these openings I could see that the city was beginning to stir. One last turn at the northeast corner and we were there.

I situated myself just outside the low wall that enclosed the market. I leaned back to wait, doing the best a freckle-faced Canadian could do to look unobtrusive. Not a chance.

Just as the golden rays of the morning sun kissed Olivet's cheek, the first ancient Volkswagen bus (one of many—it's the vehicle of choice for these shepherds, I guess) sputtered into the market. From the driver's side unfolded a heavily robed Arab. From the passenger side, usually in blue jeans and tee shirt, would jump a small, energetic representative of the next generation. Then out of the rear compartment would tumble twelve or fifteen bleating sheep, no doubt relieved to be able to breathe again.

It was the little fellows' task (the scene was repeated eight or ten times) to keep the fathers' sheep separate and localized, not an easy job. The boys were aided with sticks in each hand, sharp eyes, and boundless agility. Even then, a lamb would occasionally win the race for a few moment's freedom.

Meanwhile, the men moved about the mini-flocks, bartering for what they considered a fair price. Often the money was in and out of the folds of their garment two or three times before a deal was struck.

Sometimes the buyer wanted the animal killed. The price was the price of blood. For this purpose, there was a raised area in the corner of the enclosure with a ramp leading up to it. That morning I watched a lamb die. I do not consider myself to be squeamish. There was something, however, about the incarnadine rivulet that ran down against the tawny stones of the street that caused me to gasp. Was it the strangely familiar way in which the lamb went to its slaughter, uncomplaining? Was it the calloused way the killers went about their work?

Or was it that my cheek, tear-wet, lay hard against the cold, unfeeling stones of the walled city outside of which another Lamb died? There, too, the Lamb went ungrudgingly—no, willingly. There, too, they led Him up the rugged incline to Golgotha's brow. "And sitting down, they watched Him there."

I do not know how long I stood there looking at the scarlet pool. Long enough, certainly, to travel back two thousand years. My reverie was interrupted by someone hosing away the little lamb's life into the gutter. My watch told me it would soon be time to make for the hotel, but if I hurried, I could have a few minutes at a spot just outside the Damascus Gate. A broken outcrop, Moriah's severed northern peak. Is it the place? I think so, but no matter. I stood and looked beyond it anyway. The city swirled around me but I didn't see them.

I watched a Lamb die.

The Sheep Market

This is Not the Last Chapter

High in the Judean Hills, crouching like a lion on Moriah and Ophel and Zion, we have gazed on the City of the Great King. No rightful sovereign has ruled here for well over two thousand years. The last of Judah's monarchs was crucified outside its walls. Since then, the place has heard the somber echo of scores of marching foes through its streets, being trodden underfoot of the Gentiles. And through the centuries, Jerusalem has been the place of more weeping than any other site on earth.

David wept here; wept in remorse over sin, at the rejection of the people, in regret at the death of Absalom. Isaiah and Jeremiah wept here, mingling their tears with orphaned children, widows, distraught old men and frustrated youths. Tears of grief and loss, of bitterness and anger have stained her time-worn pavement. The Man of Sorrows wept here, too. Only He could understand the troubles that would soon encompass the City of Peace. Listen to His plaintive cry echoing across the Kidron from Olivet until it was driven back in His face by the stolid stone ramparts: "O Jerusalem, Jerusalem, which killest the prophets, and stonest them that are sent unto thee; how often would I have gathered thy children together, as a hen doth gather her brood under her wings, and ye would not!" (Lk. 13:34).

Jerome (c. 347-420) wrote: "Until this very day…it is forbidden to citizens not of the faith to come to Jerusalem…they may only come there to lament, and for the right to weep over the ruins of their houses they must pay. At no time whatsoever may they weep *gratis*." In the 13th Century, Nachmanides described the scene: "I write you this letter from the Holy City Jerusalem. Great is the suffering, and great is the devastation, and the holier the place, the greater the devastation…we found a dilapidated house…and made it into a synagogue; for the city has no ruler and anyone can, if he will, take a ruin…there are always people coming to Jerusalem…to see the temple and to weep."

Since then, the river of tears has flowed on. Israel is still a land full of weeping, and her greatest sorrows is, sadly, yet to come—the time of Jacob's Trouble (Jer. 30:7). With what relief the little sorely-tried remnant will turn their eyes heavenward to see the Sun of Righteousness arise with healing in His rays. How they shall need it. Then will Isaiah's words come to pass: "For the people shall dwell in Zion at Jerusalem: thou shalt weep no more: He will be very gracious unto thee at the voice of thy cry; when He shall hear it, He will answer thee" (Isa. 30:19).

In the meantime, trouble swirls about the little land. Turmoil and dilemmas meet her on every hand. Few of her people are desperate enough yet to look to Jehovah for His answer. And God looks down from heaven, awaiting the moment for the return of Judah's Lion.

If you cannot weep for Zion, will you pray for her? For her leaders, beset on every side, with no answers to her insuperable problems. For her suffering people, both the sons of Ishmael and Isaac. For those living there under severe pressure who seek to lift the veil a little from the hearts of some blindly groping after the Great Answer. For the dear believers and their children who are ostracized by all. For the peace of Jerusalem and for the coming of her Prince. Especially for that!

No, this is not the last chapter. We have read the Book and know how it ends. John writes: "And I…saw the holy city, new Jerusalem, coming down from God out of heaven, prepared as a bride adorned for her husband. And I heard a great voice out of heaven saying, Behold, the tabernacle of God is with men, and He will dwell with them, and they shall be His people, and God Himself shall be with them, and be their God. And God shall wipe away all tears from their eyes; and there shall be no more death, neither sorrow, nor crying, neither shall there be any more pain: for the former things are passed away…I am Alpha and Omega, the beginning and the end. I will give unto him that is athirst of the fountain of the water of life freely…But the fearful, and unbelieving…shall have their part in the lake which burneth with fire and brimstone: which is the second death" (Rev. 21:1-8). Are you on the winning side?

O lead me on to Zion's hill, to see the Lord His Word fulfill;
His glorious King is sitting there, ruling o'er earth and sea and air.

A typical street in the Old City of Jerusalem.

"At that time, will I cause the Branch of righteousness to grow up unto David; and He shall execute judgment and righteousness in the land. In those days shall Judah be saved, and Jerusalem shall dwell safely: and this is the name wherewith she shall be called, The Lord our Righteousness" (Jer. 33:15-16).

A Bibliography from My Library

Alexander, P., ed. *The Lion Encyclopedia of the Bible*. Herts, England: 1986.

Allegro, J. *The Mystery of the Dead Sea Scrolls Revealed*. New York: Gramerey Publishing Co., 1956.

Allon, Y. *My Father's House*. Translated by Reuven Ben-Yosef. New York: W. W Norton & Co., 1976.

Baly, D. *The Geography of the Bible*. New York: Harper & Brothers, 1957.

Baron, D. *The Ancient Scripture and the Modern Jew*. London: Hodder & Stoughton, 1909.

Baron, D. *Rays of Messiah's Glory*. Grand Rapids: Zondervan, undated.

Beitzel, B. J. *The Moody Atlas of Bible Lands*. Chicago: Moody Press, 1985.

Ben-Gurion, D. *Ben-Gurion Looks at the Bible*. Translated by Jonathan Kolatch. New York: Jonathan David Pub., 1972.

Ben-Gurion, D. *Israel: A Personal History*. New York: Hertzl Press, 1972.

Berrett, L. C. *Discovering the World of the Bible*. Nashville: Thomas Nelson Publishers, 1979.

Booth, A. E. *The Land Far Off*. London: Alfred Holness, no date.

Bruce, F. F. *Israel and the Nations*. Exeter: Paternoster Press, 1963.

Clapham, J. W. *Palestine: The Land of My Adoption*. London: Pickering & Inglis Ltd.,1946.

Cohn, J. H. *Beginning at usalem*. New York: American Board of Missions to the Jews, Inc. 1948.

Collins, L., and LaPierre, D. *O Jerusalem*. New York: Simon and Schuster, 1972.

Davies, A. P. *The Meaning of the Dead Sea Scrolls*. New York: Signet Books, 1956.

Dolan, D. *Holy War for the Promised Land*. Thomas Nelson, 1991.

Dowley, T., ed. *Discovering the Bible*. Basingstoke, England: 1986.

Dowley, T. *High Above the Holy Land*. London: Candle Books, 1986.

Duffield, G. P. *Handbook of Bible Lands*. Grand Rapids: Baker Book House, 1969.

Dunbar, J. *The Coming Glories of the Jewish Nation*. London: Pickering & Inglis, undated.

Edersheim, A. *The Life and Times of Jesus the Messiah*. New York: Longmans, Green, and Co., 1912.

Edersheim, A. *History of the Jewish Nation*. Grand Rapids: Baker, 1954.

Eichholz, G. *Landscapes of the Bible*. New York: Harper & Row, 1963.

Eisenberg, A. *The Great Discovery: The Story of the Dead Sea Scrolls*. New York: Abelard-Schuman Ltd., 1956.

Feinberg, C. L. *Israel—At the Center of History & Revelation*. Portland: Multnomah Press, 1980.

Flanigan, J. M. *The Footprints of the Saviour*. Grand Rapids: Gospel Folio Press, 1992.

Forder, A. *In and About Palestine*. London: R. T. S., 1919.

Free, J. P. *Archaeology and Bible History*. Wheaton: Van Kampen Press, 1950.

Friedman, T. L. *From Beirut to Jerusalem*. New York: Doubleday, 1989.

Gardner, J. L., gen. ed. *Reader's Digest Atlas of the Bible*. Pleasantville, NY: Reader's Digest Ass'n, 1981.

Gilbert, J. R. *Famous Jewish Lives*. Feltham: Hamlyn Publishing, 1970.

Glubb, J. B. *The Story of the Arab Legion*. London: Hodder & Stoughton, 1948.

Glubb, J. B. *Syria, Lebanon, Jordan*. London: Thames & Hudson, 1967.

Grayzel, S. *A History of the Jews*. New York: Mentor Books, 1968.

Grollenberg, L. H. *Shorter Atlas of the Bible*. London: Thomas Nelson and Sons Ltd., 1959.

Grosvenor, M. B., gen. ed. *Everyday Life in Bible Times*. Washington, D. C.: National Geographic, 1967.

Gulston, C. *Jerusalem: The Tragedy and the Triumph*. Grand Rapids: Zondervan, 1979.

Habermas, G. R. *Ancient Evidence for the Life of Jesus*. Nashville: Thomas Nelson, 1984.

Herzog, C. and Gichon, M. *Battles of the Bible*. New York: Random House, 1978.

Holley, J. E. & C.F. *Pictorial Profile of the Holy Land*. Westwood, NJ: Fleming H. Revell, 1959.

Hughes, R. *Travels in the Holy Land*. London: Merehurst Press, 1989.

Hurlbut, J. L. *Bible Atlas*. Chicago: Rand McNally, 1938.

Ironside, H. A. *Things Seen and Heard in Bible Lands*. Loizeaux Brothers, no date.

Isaacs, M. *Marty's Walking Tours in Biblical Jerusalem*. Jerusalem: Carta, 1980.

Kac, A. M. *The Rebirth of the State of Israel*. Chicago: Moody Press, 1958.

Katz, S. *Battleground: Fact and Fantasy in Palestine*. New York: Steimatzky Shapolsky, 1985.

Katz, S. *The Elite*. New York: Simon & Schuster Inc., 1992.

Kitchen, J. H. *Holy Fields.* London: The Paternoster Press, 1955.

Kraeling, E. G. *Bible Atlas.* New York: Rand McNally, 1966.

Layard, A. H. *Nineveh and its Remains.* London: John Murray, 1873.

Lockyer, H. *All the Messianic Prophecies of the Bible.* Grand Rapids: Zondervan, 1973.

Macduff, J. R. *Memories of Gennesaret.* London: James Nisbet & Co., 1856.

McDowell, J. *More Than A Carpenter.* Wheaton: Tyndale House Pub., 1977.

Miller, M. S. *Footprints in Palestine.* New York: Fleming H. Revell Co., 1936.

Monson, J. M. *The Land Between.* Jerusalem: Institute of Holy Land Studies, 1983.

Morse, S., gen. ed. *Israel: Modern Military Power.* New York: Military Press, 1984.

Morton, H. V. *In the Steps of the Master.* New York: Dodd, Mead & Co., 1954.

Morton, H. V. *Through Lands of the Bible.* New York: Dodd, Mead & Company, 1938.

Moskin, R. J. *Among Lions: The Battle for Jerusalem.* New York: Random House, 1982.

Müller, S. *The Preaching Tours and Missionary Labours of George Müller.* London: J. Nisbet & Co., 1889.

Naismith, A. & W. F. *God's People and God's Purpose.* Kilmarnock: John Ritchie, 1949.

Nun, M. *The Sea of Galilee and Its Fishermen in the New Testament.* Kibbutz Ein Gev: Kinnereth Sailing Co., 1989.

Olson, A. *Inside Jerusalem.* Glendale, CA: G/L Publications, 1968.

Parker, J. I, Tenney, M. C. & White, W., eds. *All the People and Places of the Bible.* Nashville: Thomas Nelson, 1982.

Payne, J. B. *An Outline of Hebrew History.* Grand Rapids: Baker, 1954.

Pearlman, M. and Yannai, Y. *Historical Sites in the Holy Land.* Valley Forge, PA: Judson Press, 1985.

Peres, S. *From These Men.* New York: Wyndham Books, 1979.

Pfeiffer, C. *Jerusalem Through the Ages.* Grand Rapids: Baker, 1967.

Phillips, J. *Exploring the World of the Jew.* Chicago: Moody Press, 1981.

Pixner, B. *With Jesus Through Galilee.* Rosh Pina: Corazin Pub., 1992.

Polano, H. *Selections from the Talmud.* London: Frederick Warne & Co., 5636 (date by Jewish reckoning).

Politeyan, J. *Biblical Discoveries in Egypt, Palestine and Mesopotamia.* London: Chas J Thynne, 1921.

Pollock, A. J. *The Amazing Jew.* London: Central Bible Truth Depot.

Potok, C. *Wanderings.* New York: Fawcett Crest, 1978.

Price, W. K. *Next Year in Jerusalem.* Chicago: Moody Press, 1975.

Rasmussen, C. G. *NIV Atlas of the Bible.* Grand Rapids: Zondervan, 1989.

Raviv, D. and Melman, Y. *Every Spy a Prince.* Boston: Houghton Mifflin, 1990.

Reich, M. I. *The Messianic Hope of Israel.* Grand Rapids: Eerdmans, 1940.

Rimmer, H. *Palestine, The Coming Storm Center.* Grand Rapids: Eerdmans, 1940.

Roberts, D. *Yesterday the Holy Land.* Grand Rapids: Zondervan, 1982.

Sale-Harrison, L. *The Remarkable Jew.* Harrisburg: Evangelical Press, 1928.

Schofield, A. T. *Where He Dwelt: Mind Pictures of Palestine.* Chicago: Rand McNally & Co., 1914.

Smith, G. A. *The Historical Geography of the Holy Land* (25th revised ed.). New York: Harper, 1966.

Steven, S. *The Spymasters of Israel.* New York: Random House, 1980.

St. John, R. *Ben Gurion: The Biography of an Extraordinary Man.* Garden City, NY: Doubleday & Co, 1959.

St. John, R. *Tongue of the Prophets: The Life of Eliezer Ben Yehuda.* New York: Doubleday & Co., 1952.

Trever, J. C. *The Dead Sea Scrolls: A Personal Account.* Grand Rapids: Eerdmans, 1965.

Thompson, J. A. *Handbook of Life in Bible Times.* Leicester, England: Inter-Varsity Press, 1986.

Unger, M. F. *Archaeology and the New Testament.* Grand Rapids: Zondervan, 1962.

Van Deursen, A. *Illustrated Dictionary of Bible Manners and Customs.* New York: Philosophical Library, Inc., 1967.

Van Dyke, H. *Out-Of-Doors in the Holy Land.* New York: Charles Scribner's Sons, 1908.

Vester, B. S. *Our Jerusalem.* New York: Arno Press, 1977.

Vester, B. S. *Flowers of the Holy Land.* Kansas City: Hallmark Cards, 1964.

Wright, G. E. *Great People of the Bible and How They Lived.* Pleasantville, NY: Reader's Digest Ass'n, 1974.

Zohary, M. *Plants of the Bible.* Cambridge: Cambridge University Press, 1982.

Thomson, W. M. *The Land and the Book.* Grand Rapids: Baker, 1954.

Walker, W. *All the Plants of the Bible.* New York: Harper & Brothers, 1957.

Waters, A. L. and Marsh, K. A. *Journey to the Land of Jesus.* Publications International, 1992.

Sunrise over the Sea of Galilee. Here about this lake the One who became poor for us slept on the hillsides. He could say, "The foxes have holes, the birds of the air have nests, but the Son of man hath not where to lay His head."

Scripture Index